BUS

Business as Usual

The Economic Crisis and the Failure of Capitalism

Paul Mattick

REAKTION BOOKS

Published by Reaktion Books Ltd
33 Great Sutton Street
London
EC IV ODX

www.reaktionbooks.co.uk

First published 2011
Copyright © Paul Mattick 2011

Printed and bound in Great Britain
by Bell & Bain, Glasgow

British Library Cataloguing in Publication Data
Mattick, Paul, 1944–
Business as Usual : The Economic Crisis and the Failure of Capitalism.
1. Global Financial Crisis, 2008–2009.
2. Business cycles.
3. Economic history – 1945–
4. Capitalism.
I. Title
338.5'42-dc22

ISBN 978 1 86189 801 2

Contents

Well, it's not just me
And it's not just you
This is all around the world.

— PAUL SIMON

Preface

When the American financial system began to unravel in late 2007, sending trillions of dollars up in smoke, not only politicians but most experts, from the halls of academe to newspaper financial pages, agreed that though things might be serious, comparisons to the Great Depression were un-called for. A few months later, however, that comparison was everywhere, if only as background for insistence that this time the downward spiral could be controlled – provided that governments did the right thing, and fast. (Otherwise, as the then leader of the free world put it, 'This sucker's going down.') Three years later, the worst seems to have been avoided, and what has been dubbed the Great Recession is generally supposed to be giving way to recovery. This recovery, however, seems to be of the jobless variety, with banks still reluctant to extend much credit and successive fiscal crises in Europe and elsewhere doing nothing to counter un-ease in the world's financial markets.

Only a few years ago, economists who explained the rational, efficient, self-correcting nature of the market system were winning Nobel prizes; those who disagreed with them were sure that proper government policies would make up for whatever limits to growth capitalism might bump up against. Both of these versions of economic orthodoxy have been more difficult to believe since the economic gains of yester-year melted away like glaciers under the impact of global warming, as fortunes vanished from stock markets around the world and the nine largest US banks lost more money in three weeks of early 2008 than they made in profit during the three years after 2004, while governments struggled to contain the damage. And yet, despite the surprising readiness of publications like *The Economist* (which, on 18 October 2008, featured a story on 'Capitalism at Bay') to consider the economic system as truly imperilled by its current disorder, it is still difficult for people to understand that the current crisis is the result of more than greed, corporate irresponsibility and the deregulation of financial markets. Greed and corporate irresponsibility are hardly novel features of capitalist society. And if the dismantling of the regulations put in place in the United States during and after the Great Depression to limit financial hijinks eased the way both to fraud and to the extension of speculation beyond sustainable limits, it is also what made possible the exuberant expansion of credit on which the level of well-being achieved over the last two decades depended. Understanding the Great Recession requires looking beyond the contributions made to the debacle by governmental connivance and the instability inherent in newfangled financial contrivances like the now infamous collateralized debt obligations and credit default swaps, to the long-term dynamic of capitalism itself.

This book attempts to understand the present-day state of affairs by setting it in the context of that long-term dynamic. Doing this, of course, requires making judgements about which aspects of the past are most relevant to understanding the present and speculating about the future. The failure of economic theory to predict or even explain the story so far should, to put it mildly, give us pause before we take the pronouncements of its quarrelling practitioners too seriously. So the approach taken here starts with the conclusion James K. Galbraith recently drew from wide knowledge of his academic profession: that it is 'pointless to continue with conversations centred on the conventional economics'.[1] Instead I draw upon the thinking of Karl Marx, who described himself not as an economist but as a critic of economic theory.

Marx lived a long time ago, and capitalism has changed in important ways since he wrote about it. But his theorizing operated on such a high plane of abstraction that it is still relevant to the economic system we live in today.[2] Marx's abstractions, moreover, are different from those of conventional economics, which claim to apply across history: Marx emphasized those features of modern society that make capitalism different from other social systems. Hence his focus on the role of money in economic affairs, and in particular on the need of businesses to make profit, central both to a general understanding of the alternation of prosperity and depression and, as we will see, to grasping the limits of economic policy when, as at the present time, governments attempt to move an economy in trouble back to recovery. My confidence in this mode of analysis has been strengthened by the fact that since the start of the crisis in 2007 I have correctly anticipated the ways in which it has continued to unfold, in contrast to most professional commentators. This is not because I am smarter than other people, and it has been true despite my having less access to data than most professional economists; it is a matter of knowing how to think about what is going on. This is what I want to share with readers.

While this book thus does not avoid theory, because reality cannot be understood without it, I have made an effort to avoid jargon of any sort. I assume neither great acquaintance with economics nor much knowledge of economic history on the reader's part; my wish is to supply just enough of both to make sense of ongoing events. I do not spend much time discussing alternative approaches (unavoidable or irresistible comments in this vein are for the most part confined to footnotes), beyond discussion of the dominant modes of economic theory insofar as they have influenced economic policy. Historical data is for the most part drawn from official sources. The limits to the accuracy of such data are well known, or ought to be; though we have to use them, because they are all there is, exact numbers for things like growth rates or unemployment should be taken with a pinch of salt.[3]

I

What Happened?

How are we to describe the events that have convulsed the global economy since 2007? Almost everyone seems to agree that there was a financial crisis, which gave rise to a recession. While the latter is commonly described as the worst since the Great Depression, the widely held view is that swift action by the US government to bail out financial corporations averted the threat of depression, opening the way for the 'green shoots' of recovery discerned already at the end of summer 2009 by Federal Reserve chairman Ben Bernanke.[1] Some economists and journalists did not expect full economic bloom until another year or two, while almost all agreed that even an improved economy would take the form of a 'jobless recovery'. But the consensus view, when I finished writing this book in mid-2010, was that we were already on the way out of what had come to be called, ruefully, the Great Recession – a view officially confirmed by the Business Cycle Dating Committee of the National Bureau of Economic Research when it announced in September 2010 that the recession had ended fifteen months earlier.

There was general agreement as well about the causes of the collapse of the American finance industry that set the global downturn in motion: this collapse was an unintended consequence (though perhaps an expectable one, even if most economists and financiers did not expect it) of unparalleled financial risk-taking, stimulated by the fantastic profits achieved by this sector in the 1990s, helped along by lax governmental regulation. This line of thinking points, for example, to the enormous salaries and bonuses reaped by professional speculators working at banks, hedge funds and other financial enterprises, which gave them an incentive to risk their firms' money, and especially other people's money borrowed by their firms, to pursue short-term profits to the limits allowed by government regulators (and even beyond). Thus, to cite a particularly simple-minded example, the Nobel-prize-winning economics professor Paul Krugman used his column in the *New York Times* to opine that 'reforming bankers' compensation is the single best thing we can do to prevent another financial crisis a few years down the road'.[2]

Although over-leveraged, risk-taking speculation was an international phenomenon, the heart of the problem lay in the United States, the world's dominant economy and financial centre. Here the traders' risky behaviour had a home in what is commonly described as a culture of self-indulgent high living. As individuals, too many Americans borrowed too much money; too many banks made loans to unreliable customers. The danger inherent in this situation was magnified by a technical innovation that was supposed to manage risk by spreading it, the 'securitization' of mortgages and other types of loan – their grouping together into bundles sold as bonds. In this way the bank that makes the loans doesn't tie up its money in an actual piece of property, waiting for the loan to be repaid, but sells the right to collect the interest on those mortgages (or, for example, credit card accounts) to investors – other banks, pension funds and so on – in complexly structured packages called 'collateralized debt obligations'. The investors, of course, can sell these CDOs to others, or use them as collateral to take out giant loans to buy more securities or to gamble in the rapidly expanding field of derivatives, a type of investment well described in the *Financial Times* as 'like putting a mirror in front of another mirror, allowing a physical object to be reflected into infinity'; about $62 trillion in credit default swap derivatives, for example, were floating around when the crisis hit. By January 2007, the US mortgage-based bonds on which this inverted pyramid of financial instruments rested, themselves rising far from actual houses and the money to be paid for them, had a total value of $5.8 trillion. Of this, 14 per cent represented sub-prime mortgages, entered into by people with poor financial resources. In 2006 these people began to have a hard time making their payments and the pyramid fractured.

The foreclosure wave should not have been surprising, as the real wages of non-supervisory workers in the US had reached their peak in the early 1970s and stagnated since then (the years after 2000 saw in particular a rapid decline in employer-financed health insurance), along with employment. When variable mortgage payments jumped, more and more people couldn't make them. Meanwhile, the Fed raised interest rates starting in 2004. The same institution's earlier lowering of interest rates had encouraged borrowing, including for speculative purposes. As they went up, mortgages became more expensive, houses were harder to sell and house prices stalled or fell. These developments in turn made it difficult or impossible to refinance, as many homebuyers had been assured by lenders they would be able to do. By December 2007 nearly a million US households were facing foreclosure. Housing prices began to fall more rapidly; the mortgage market collapsed, taking with it the whole structure of securitized investments, now a massive part of the financial structure in the US and around the world.

Alan S. Blinder, former Federal Reserve Bank governor and now Krugman's fellow professor at Princeton University, put it this way: 'It's easy to forget amid all the fancy stuff – credit derivatives, swaps – that the root cause of all this is declining house prices.' People, from humble homeowners to Wall Street Masters of the Universe, imagined that house prices would climb forever. When they started to fall, the institutions that bought mortgages and borrowed against them, treating them as the equivalent of high-valued houses, suddenly found themselves unable to meet their obligations. Because so many institutions had become embroiled in the mortgage market by buying securitized mortgages, the effect on the whole financial system was swift and deadly: as more and more payments could not be met, more collateral was demanded to back up borrowings, which further depressed the institutions' ability to manoeuvre. Major banks were forced into mergers or bankruptcy, while the insurance giant American International Group, which had insured billions of dollars' worth of these transactions, survived only thanks to a massive injection of US government funds. Bank credit became unavailable – and capitalism lives on credit, required not only by individuals rolling over their monthly credit-card bills but by businesses of all sizes meeting weekly payrolls and other operating expenses. In short order, there-fore, the financial crisis – in this account – produced the Great Recession.

A more complex version of this story invokes a global dimension: the American economic expansion of recent dec-ades, after all, involved a growing trade and current-accounts deficit in relation to the rest of the world. Americans bought more goods from the rest of the world than they produced to sell. And the money they spent flowed back to the USA, invested in stocks, bonds and real estate, but also in the government securities that, in a circle that was vicious or virtuous depending on one's point of view, financed the persistent outflow of dollars to buy goods from around the world. This inflow helped keep American interest rates low, allowing people to buy foreign-made goods as well as to take out mortgages and purchase houses and apartments. While many nations were involved in this, the Chinese government became the largest holder of US Treasury bonds, thus financing the growing appetite for Chinese-made goods on the part of American consumers and keeping the prices of those goods low (since the massive flow of dollars into China would otherwise have pushed up the value of the Chinese currency, the renminbi,[3] making Chinese goods more expensive on the world market). Thus China, and the other major dollar-hoarding countries, enabled (as they say in rehab) the American consumption habit, and with it the debt expansion and hypertrophied speculation that led to the financial collapse. In the words of a leading columnist for the *Financial Times*, Martin Wolf,

> High-income countries with elastic credit systems and households willing to take on rising debt levels offset the massive surplus savings in the rest of the world. The lax monetary policies facilitated this excess spending, while the housing bubble was the vehicle through which it worked.[4]

Conversely, once the financial system seized up in the United States, it was bound to spread throughout a world in which national economies are knitted together by financial and trade flows.

All of this makes sense, as far as it goes, and corresponds to phenomena apparent to anyone reading the financial pages of the world's mainstream newspapers. The outstanding issues seem to be those of what to do next. What sorts of reforms of the financial system are necessary (and possible)? Is more stimulus money needed in one nation or another to fully prime the economic pump or has enough been spent already? What measures should be taken to aid the unemployed and maintain state services while the economy returns to normal? John E. Silvia, chief economist for Wells Fargo, expressed the most optimistic version of this perspective in a 'research note' published in the *New York Times* on 29 July 2009: 'The recession is over, the economy is recovering – let's look forward and stop the backward-looking focus.'

A Crisis in Economics

In taking this stance, Silvia only affirmed his faith in the currently dominant strain of economic theory. According to the leading economists of the last thirty years, the financial transactions that played such a central role in the current debacle are an efficient mechanism for allocating resources among potential uses. The same Martin Wolf who now laments a fundamental imbalance in the world economy saw a means for stability in global financial flows in 2004, his only caveat being that 'if some people (Asians) wish to spend less than they earn today, then others need to be encouraged to spend more'.[5] Meanwhile, what was in fact, in historical terms, a relatively stagnant economy, moving through recessions of various degrees of severity and undergoing an unending series of banking, debt and currency crises, was described as essentially stable. Thus Nobel Prize winner Robert E. Lucas Jr wrote in the *Wall Street Journal* – in late 2007, when real-estate finance was already disintegrating – that he was

> skeptical about the argument that the subprime mortgage problem will contaminate the whole mortgage market, that housing construction will come to a halt, and that the economy will slip into a recession. Every step in this chain is questionable and none has been quantified. If we have learned anything from the past 20 years it is that there is a lot of stability built into the real economy.[6]

What perturbations there were, according to this vision of capitalism, could originate only from outside the economic mechanism proper – above all from mistaken government regulative, fiscal and monetary policy.

In this way, at the turn of the twenty-first century economics reaffirmed the rosy view of the private-enterprise system that had characterized the field in its earliest days. Throughout the nineteenth century, economic orthodoxy maintained that the natural state of a capitalist economy was a healthy full employment of resources to produce the maximum amount of goods for consumption. After all, as Adam Smith had already explained in *The Wealth of Nations* (1776), the whole point of a capitalist economy is that each individual owes his or her living to success in meeting the needs of others. Only what can be sold will be produced; money will be borrowed, land rented and labour hired only because the resulting production meets a need. Conversely, the money earned by selling one's product will be spent, either on consumption or on further production. David Ricardo, the great systematizer of early nineteenth-century theory, portrayed the economy as tending naturally to a balanced state, in which all products found buyers, with goods selling at 'natural' prices. True, Ricardo saw trouble ahead for capitalism, but only because population growth would require the cultivation of increasingly infertile land; the diversion of wealth away from entrepreneurs to landlords that would eventually limit growth was the fault of physical nature, not the economy. As the idea of capitalism's self-regulation was expressed by Ricardo's follower J. B. Say, 'supply creates its own demand'. Since there's no way of knowing in advance how much of each kind of product will be consumed, there can be momentary imbalances between supply and demand, but the rise and fall of prices will see to it that the necessary adjustments are made.

In the later nineteenth century the 'classical' political economy of Smith, Ricardo, and their followers was replaced by a new 'neoclassical' mode of theorizing that was in many ways quite different. It emphasized not, like classical theory, the division of income among social classes, but the decision-making of individuals. Borrowing the concept of 'equilibrium' from physics, along with the mathematics of static mechanics, the new economics continued to insist that capitalism by its nature tended to settle in a stable state in which each individual is maximally satisfied, given the constraints set by his or her relations to the rest of the system. (How this idea was to be reconciled with the equally basic dogma that capitalism tends to grow as a wealth-producing system was left for future thinkers to resolve.) From this point of view too, therefore, breakdowns of the market system, as opposed to imbalances in particular markets, are out of the question; what general difficulties do occur must be the effects of some non-economic factor, such as the weather, human psychology or mistaken government policies.

The Great Depression that began in 1929 (that name had previously been assigned to the downturn that lasted from 1873 to 1896) finally made it possible for the fiction of natural stability and perpetual growth to be questioned by a figure as institutionally important as John Maynard Keynes, financial representative of the British government at the Versailles conference to end the First World War, professor of economics at Cambridge and all-round leading light of British intellectual life. In his *General Theory of Employment, Interest, and Money* of 1936 Keynes observed that the insistence of orthodox economics on the self-regulated nature of the capitalist economy had failed to recognize that the system could regulate itself into a state of less than full employment. Sharing with orthodoxy the basic assumption that the point of the economy is the utilization of resources, natural and human, to produce goods for consumption, Keynes proposed that the state should intervene at such moments, borrowing money against future tax receipts to hire workers, thus increasing the number of consumers and so calling forth new investment to meet their needs. Like his predecessors, Keynes ascribed the possibility of breakdown to a non-economic factor, human psychology, which limited the ability of the growth of consumption to keep up with the ability to produce, along with a pattern of expectations, ideally based on experience, about the profits to be earned from investment. But as humans cause the problem, humans could repair it, with government policy undoing the psychologically set limits on full employment and prosperity. This is the origin of the concept of the 'stimulus' – the idea that the economy need only be nudged to a different supply–demand equilibrium position for its natural tendency to stabilize to operate at a higher level of employment and consumption.

In 1936, when Keynes published his book, the idea that government spending should make up for the shortfall in capital investment and consumer demand had already been put into practice by governments as different as Adolf Hitler's and Franklin Delano Roosevelt's. By the end of the Second World War, the massive military expenditures required had restored high levels of employment and improved the general standard of living, at least in the United States. This gave an enormous boost to the fortunes of Keynesianism (if not precisely to Keynes's own ideas, as many of Keynes's theoretical disciples pointed out over the decades, without making much political or academic headway[7]). Depressions now seemed to be something that could be controlled and even avoided altogether.

Interestingly enough, the loss of faith in Keynesian theory that came with the return of economic stagnation in the 1970s, now accompanied by inflation, led not to a search for new ways to grapple with the nature of the 'business cycle' of alternating contractions and expansions, but to a renewed insistence that the market, if only left to itself, would provide the best of all economic worlds. In economic practice, government stimulus of the economy reached a postwar high point under Ronald Reagan, apostle of the free market and battler against the Evil Empire of the Soviet Union's state-run economic system. In economic theory, however, the period since the late 1970s saw the dominance of the field by insistence on various forms of the efficient-market hypothesis. Originating in nineteenth-century studies of the probabilistic nature of business decision-making, this is the idea that stock market prices provide the best available estimates of the real value of shares, and so of the actual state of business enterprises, because 'the market' – that is, the bargaining conducted between all buyers and sellers – takes account of all available information in setting the price of an individual stock. The hypothesis thus extended to asset markets – markets for stocks, real estate, commodity futures and other vehicles for speculative investment (including, for example, CDOs) – the assumptions about the self-equilibrating nature of commodity markets basic to the classical theory of *laissez-faire*.

The degree of dominance that this view achieved within economic discourse in recent decades guaranteed a radical crisis of faith in economic theory when the financial house of cards came tumbling down. 'What Good Are Economists Anyway?' asked *Business Week*'s cover story for 16 April 2009, noting that though the world is 'simply too complicated' for 'exactitude' in prediction, it is distressing that 'seven decades after the Depression, economists still haven't reached consensus on its lessons'. An even harsher rebuke came from within the profession when Paul Krugman asked, in the pages of the *New York Times Magazine*, 'How Did Economists Get It So Wrong?' Despite his title, Krugman did not have all economists in mind, but only those who followed recent neoclassical fashion (he left undiscussed the reasons why Keynesian theory fell into disrepute in the 1970s). Locating 'the central cause of the profession's failure' in 'the desire for an all-encompassing, intellectually elegant approach that also gave economists a chance to show off their mathematical prowess', Krugman dismissed the approaches dominating academic economics over the last 30 years as fundamentally misguided and called for a return to Keynesian theory as part of a recognition of the fundamental 'messiness' of the economy.[8] Writing in the *Financial Times*, Robert Skidelsky (best known for his authoritative biography of Keynes) similarly noted that the efficient-market hypothesis's collision with the iceberg of economic reality had 'led to the discrediting of mainstream macroeconomics' and given the lie to economists' claim to practice a predictive science.[9]

Such shock at the predictive failure of economics is surprising, given the dismal record of professional forecasting. The enthusiasm spawned after the Second World War by the apparent success of economists in understanding and managing the economy led many companies to hire in-house forecasters in the 1950s and '60s. But 'thanks to the poor historical performance of economic forecasting', today 'almost none of the Fortune 500 companies directly employ economists. Instead, they avoid relying on forecasts altogether . . .'.[10] Clearly, economics is neither a reliable predictive science nor a body of theory on whose basics practitioners can agree. Yet *Business Week*'s writer, Peter Coy, Krugman and Skidelsky could think of no alternative to further theoretical heavy lifting by the economics profession.

For the most part, as we have seen, even those attempting to face up to the current debacle of economic practice and theory continue to accept the basic dogma of the now discredited approach to economics: the idea of an essentially problem-free nature of capitalism, apart from financial excesses. In the words of George Cooper – a professional fund manager whose recent book reflecting on the crisis-prone nature of the financial system makes a merciless mockery of the efficient-market hypothesis – the 'markets for goods and services' are characterized by 'stability' but this does 'not hold for asset markets, credit markets, and the capital market system in general', which once disequilibrated have no tendency to return to an equilibrium state.[11] The problem, that is, is not the capitalist economy as such, the production and distribution for profit of goods and services – often referred to as the 'real economy' – but the financial superstructure erected on its basis which, allowed to get out of control, can unravel with consequences for the underlying structure itself. Even some left-wing thinkers, who one might have imagined would be only too happy to proclaim new evidence of capitalism's obsolescence, chimed in with this strand of the mainstream chorus.[12]

Other leftists explain the recession by combining the generally noted fragility of the financial structure with the Keynesian diagnosis of insufficient effective demand. Thus David Harvey's recent book on economic crisis explains the current downturn as the outcome of earlier efforts to maintain capitalist prosperity by lowering the high wages earned by workers in the 1960s:

Moves made to alleviate a crisis of labour supply and to curb the political power of organized labour in the 1970s diminished the effective demand for the product [of industry], which created difficulties for realization of [profit] in the market during the 1990s. Moves to alleviate this last problem by extensions of the credit system among the working classes ultimately led to working-class over-indebtedness relative to income that in turn led to a crisis of confidence in the quality of debt instruments (as began to happen in 2006).[13]

But if the Great Recession developed from a financial crisis, why is the world economy still slowing, even as bailouts to the financial system, together with stimuli administered to the general economy, are supposedly producing 'green shoots' of recovery? Why will this recovery be a job-less one, thus requiring (as Keynesians of various ideological stripes, from Krugman to Harvey, maintain) government spending to revive demand and increase employment? In the US, when these words were written in spring 2010, big bonuses were back in the financial world, but wages were not going up, to put it mildly, while the average work week declined and unemployment continued to rise. The remaining investment houses were making excellent profits on financial trades, while banks remained unwilling to offer credit to businesses that need it to survive, let alone expand. General Motors, near bankruptcy in 2008, has been saved, apparently, by government action, at the cost of huge numbers of jobs, while those still on the payroll have had to accept lower wage, health and pension terms. But the corporation's home state of Michigan – along with California, the largest state in the union – was sliding into fiscal collapse, closing universities, schools and libraries while cutting basic services like healthcare. Meanwhile, the European economy continued to slow, with rising unemployment, while Japan remained mired in stagnation. China, it is true, reported growth, at the spectacular rate of 9.1 per cent for 2009. This was no doubt due in part to the continuing ability of Chinese industry to take market share from producers in other countries, thanks to a mixture of government subsidies, continued maintenance of a cheap currency and the efficacy of a police state in keeping wages low and working conditions harsh (despite some limited success of recent workers' protests and strikes). But it clearly owed much to the 4 trillion renminbi ($590 billion) pumped into the economy by the state, along with a record 9.6 trillion renminbi ($1.4 trillion) of bank debt, much of it channelled into real-estate speculation. The artificial character of this 'growth', in fact, was such as to prompt official worries 'that the stimulus drove overspending on factories and other facilities, which could lead to economic problems if producers were forced to slash prices in glutted markets or could not repay bank loans', not to mention the ripening real-estate development bubble.[14]

If we disobey John Silvia and allow ourselves a backward-looking look, we are faced with the question of just how the imbalance in the world economy implicated in the financial meltdown came to pass in the first place. To start with the last-mentioned thread of the story, why did the Chinese government (and other East Asian and Middle Eastern nations) facilitate the American housing bubble, with all the financial hijinks it involved, by buying Treasury bonds rather than, say, using their dollars to invest in American industry? Of course, as already noted, this helped solidify their foreign exchange position, protecting the value of their currency. And there would have been little point in financing US production when the basis of developing Chinese capitalism is the replacement of the US as a centre of production. But why did the American economy decline as an engine of production rather than consumption? Why did investment slow in the US, outside of the stock and bond markets, real estate and derivatives, so that by 2007 so-called financial services earned a historically high 28.3 per cent of total corporate profits? Between 2000 and 2005, as one commentator emphasizes, 'the increase of both non-residential investment and net exports was *less than zero*, so that personal consumption and residential investment' – both based on mortgage-debt expansion – 'were left the drive the economy virtually by themselves'.[15]

And since this is not only an American story, why was the world economy increasingly devoted to speculative pursuits? How did what were once called 'developing countries' turn into 'developing markets', with an emphasis on securities, real estate and commodity futures speculation? Even in China, which has been busy turning out everything from steel to teddy bears, vast sums of money have poured into real-estate development, producing a growing bubble that had experts worried before more immediate problems distracted them. It was, as we shall see, largely this worldwide growth in financial activity after 1980 that appeared both as 'globalization' and as the American prosperity supposedly powering the world economy. Conversely, the crisis appeared as a financial crisis, not because the rest of the economy was healthy, but because finance was the most dynamic sector of the economy, and therefore the one in which the underlying weakness first manifested itself.

Clearly there is something wrong with the mainstream approach to understanding current economic affairs. Part of the problem lies in the terms with which commentators attempt to understand the social system in which we live. These analytic difficulties are inextricably connected with insufficient attention to the actual course of economic events. To understand what happened and what is still happening in the world economy, we need to take a longer view than that which seemed to support the enthusiasm of recent economic theory. We need to look back at history – the history of capitalism as a system, and the history of this system since the Second World War in particular.

2

Ups and Downs

A remarkable feature of the commentary on today's economic troubles is that despite constant reference to the Great Depression of the 1930s, as well as to the downturns since the Second World War (particularly the relatively severe recession of 1981), there has been little mention of the fact that business depressions have been a recurrent feature of the capitalist economy. But even the briefest attention to history makes recent events appear considerably less unusual. Major downturns have been identified in every decade from the 1820s forward, increasing steadily in seriousness up to the Big One in 1929. In 1835, for instance, the *National Gazette* reported on the speculative boom set off in the United States by the expansion in trade made possible by the westward extension of canals and railroads (the value of New York City real estate increased 150 per cent between 1830 and 1837). Speculation

> in stocks and real property is more general and extravagant than it has been before . . . in all our principal cities . . . [M]ultitudes are now prominent and desperate dealers in the stock and other speculation markets, of classes and ages, callings and positions in life, that formerly were never seen nor expected, and themselves never thought of acting, in such scenes . . . They chase bubbles not less intently than those who have leisure and money to spare.[1]

By 1837, bank failures had led to a collapse of domestic and external trade. 'Business firms failed by the hundreds, and workers were turned away from factory doors. In the West and South thousands of farmers lost their lands. Paper fortunes were wiped out overnight.'[2] The post-Civil War growth of American industrial capitalism led to even more serious downturns. In 1893, notably, 'some 500 banks and 16,000 business firms had been financially ruined', ushering in a deep depression, with a 25 per cent decline in economic activity and unemployment of 15 to 20 per cent, setting off widespread social unrest.[3]

From the early 1800s to the late 1930s, in fact, capitalism experienced depressions during between a third and a half of its history (depending on how they are dated by different authorities).[4] Sometimes, as in 1847–51, they gave rise to significant social upheavals; at other times, as in 1857–9, the disruption of life and the suffering they occasioned awoke little political response. Overall, they became deeper and longer over this period. In the decades after the recovery from the Great Depression of 1929–39,[5] however, the relative shallowness of economic fluctuations encouraged even those who did research into the economy's ups and downs to ignore the potential for social disruption demonstrated in earlier recessions. Todd Knoop's recent textbook on the subject goes so far as to conclude that 'the study of depressions is a somewhat different topic than the study of business cycles in general'. It is from this perspective that Knoop, in a striking denial of the facts of history, describes the depression of the 1930s as 'unprecedented',[6] and that so many economists could find the current depression so unexpected and difficult to explain.

This is a reversion to the earliest mode of study of depressions, which saw them as isolated events, each with its own explanation. By the later nineteenth century, however, it was understood that crises were part of a recurrent cycle of events, which has to be understood as such, rather than as a series of unrelated phenomena. In every case the crisis led to a recession, marked by a decline in industrial production, rising unemployment, falling wages (and other prices) and failures of financial institutions, preceded or followed by financial panics and credit crunches; in every case, the downturn was eventually followed by a return to greater levels of production (and employment) than before. Thus the idea of economic crisis evolved into recognition of what in English went under the names of the 'trade cycle' or 'business cycle', a pattern of events which, given its constant repetition, was clearly endemic to modern society.

The seventeenth and eighteenth centuries had already experienced financial panics in the European cities – London, Paris, Amsterdam – in which the growing importance of money in social life had led to the development of stock markets and other modes of finance. (A notable example was the collapse of the market in tulip bulbs in Amsterdam in 1637, the first recorded bubble.) But something new emerged when an increasingly money-centred economy gave rise to the Industrial Revolution and the establishment of capitalism in wide enough swathes of territory for it to become the dominant social system: crises of the social system as a whole. Before that, of course, social production and consumption were disrupted by a variety of disturbances: war, plague, bad harvests. But the coming of capitalism brought something new: starvation alongside good harvests and mountains of food; idle factories and unemployed workers in peacetime despite need for the goods they produced. Such breakdowns in the normal process of production, distribution and consumption were now due not to natural or political causes but to specifically *economic* factors: lack of money to purchase needed goods, profits too low to make production worthwhile.

At first only the most capitalistically developed nations were affected (the 1825 crisis took in only Great Britain and the United States). But over the next hundred years, as capitalism spread across the world and countries were increasingly linked by trade and capital movements, the cycle of crisis, recession, recovery and prosperity took in ever more areas, although not all experienced these phases in the same way, to the same extent or at the same moment. By the end of the nineteenth century, the alternation of prosperity and depression was disturbing enough to demand attention from social analysts, even if there was little room for it in the accepted frameworks of theoretical economics.

In 1860, the French Académie des Sciences Morales et Politiques sponsored a competition to 'Inquire into the causes, and indicate the effects of commercial crises that took place in Europe and North America during the XIX Century . . . As commercial relations have expanded, the perturbations crises bring with them are also touching more and more regions.'[7] The prize was won by Clément Juglar, who demonstrated the regularity of cycles on the basis of extensive statistical research. A physician by profession, Juglar mobilized concepts of normality and systemic disturbance to demonstrate that crises, despite their individual features, followed a recurrent cycle of phases suggesting that 'crises, like illnesses', are 'one of the conditions of existence of societies in which commerce and industry dominate'.[8] Seventy years later, despite a voluminous series of articles, pamphlets and books devoted to the topic, the absence of a generally accepted theory led the Assembly of the League of Nations – in view of 'the persistence with which depressions occur' and 'the gravity of their economic and social effects' – to sponsor a major study of prosperity and depression,[9] which came out in the midst of the most serious economic collapse in history.

Because both classical and neoclassical thinking had no theoretical room for systemic breakdowns, it was heterodox thinkers who did the pioneering research into the boom-bust cycle. J.-C.-L. Simonde de Sismondi, the initiator of business-cycle theory, wrote his *New Principles of Political Economy* (1819) in response to the doubts raised in his mind about the ideas of Adam Smith by 'the business crisis Europe had experienced in the last few years; the cruel sufferings of the factory workers I witnessed in Italy, Switzerland and France, and which all public accounts showed to be equally severe in England, Germany and Belgium.'[10] Sismondi came up with many of the explanations appealed to by other theorists since his time: the unplanned nature of the vast market economy; the fact that consumers' income is less than the value of goods produced; the related idea that more is invested in production than is justified by the extent of the market; and the unequal distribution of income.

Some of these ideas were also advanced, at around the same time, by Thomas Malthus, unconvinced by Ricardo's insistence that a general crisis of the economic system (as opposed to temporary disequilibria) is simply impossible. These thoughts – ancestors of many subsequent 'disproportionality', 'under-consumption' and 'overproduction' theories of crisis – draw their plausibility from the fact that in a market economy decisions about where to invest money and about what is produced, and in what quantities, are made prior to finding out what quantities of particular goods are actually wanted by consumers, and at what price. This seems obviously relevant to recurrent fluctuations in economic activity, in which different parts of a complex system adjust to each other over time. Another basic aspect of capitalism – that in order for profit to exist, the total money value of goods produced must be greater than the total money paid out in wages – suggests an inherent imbalance between production and eventual consumption. As both of these are constant features of this society, however, it is hard to see how they can explain the alternation between periods of growth and collapses serious enough, on occasion, to give large numbers of people the idea that the system was actually breaking down.

The most important, and most unorthodox, writer to tackle the question of the business cycle was Karl Marx. The nature and causes of economic crisis, and of the relation of crisis to prosperity, are central themes running through the thousands of pages he devoted to the 'critique of political economy' of which he published a single volume in 1867 under the title *Capital* (materials for the remaining volumes were edited and published by others after his death). Marx argued that capitalism's basic nature produced a tendency to crisis, which was realized in recurring depressions and would eventually bring the downfall of the system. Marx's approach differed so fundamentally from the generality of economic theorizing, however, that it proved difficult for others interested in the subject (including most of those who called themselves Marxists) even to understand his ideas, much less find them useful.

The year 1867 saw another attempt at explaining the economic cycle, an article in which English economist John Mills found its cause in the changing emotional states of investors, which swing wildly from optimism to pessimism and back. This idea has had a long life, in many different forms (Juglar, for instance, emphasized the over-optimism of investors in a period of prosperity); its most recent revival, widely hailed as a novel contribution to economic theory, is George Akerlof's and Robert Schiller's book *Animal Spirits: How Human Psychology Drives the Economy, and Why It Matters for Global Capitalism* (2009).[11] Other thinkers found the cause of the cycle in the weather, as in William Stanley Jevons's dogged efforts, starting with a publication in 1875, to prove a correlation between business ups and downs and the sunspot cycle, which he believed influenced agricultural yields and so the general state of the economy.

As these examples suggest, a common theme in business cycle theorizing has been the location of the origin of depressions outside the economic system proper; this approach remains basic to contemporary cycle theory, which seeks origins in 'exogenous shocks', and particularly in mistaken government policies. Thus Christina Romer, the first head of President Obama's Council of Economic Advisors, has written that

> there is no reason why cycles have to occur at all. The prevailing view among economists is that there is a level of economic activity, often referred to as full employment [of all inputs to the production process], at which the economy could stay forever . . . If nothing disturbs the economy, the full-employment level of output, which naturally tends to grow as the population increases and new technologies are discovered, can be maintained forever . . . Business cycles do occur, however, because disturbances . . . push the economy above or below full employment.

By 'disturbances' she means such phenomena as substantial rises or falls in government spending and waves of optimism or pessimism among consumers or firms.[12]

In an earlier day, however, Gottfried von Haberler had concluded from his 1937 survey of business-cycle theories and history for the League of Nations that crises 'cannot be accounted for by such "external" causes as bad harvests due to weather conditions, general strikes, lock-outs, earthquakes, the sudden obstruction of international trade channels and the like'. Finding this 'mysterious' – because of a presumed 'inherent tendency of the economic system towards equilibrium' that he, like Professor Romer, accepted as a feature of capitalism – Haberler defined depressions as 'those prolonged and conspicuous falls in the volume of production, real income and employment which can only be explained by the operation of factors originating within the economic system itself, and in the first instance by an insufficiency of monetary demand and the absence of a sufficient margin between price and cost'.[13] These two factors are obviously related, as a restricted market puts downward pressure on prices and so limits the price for which goods, whose costs were determined at an earlier moment, can be sold.

In the efforts made by researchers to follow Juglar's example by studying quantities of statistical materials, the theoretical biases of the German Historical School and the Institutionalism of Thorstein Veblen and his followers in the United States played an important role: both emphasized social-historical facts as a basis for understanding the economy, in contrast to the high level of mathematicized abstraction favoured by the neoclassical mainstream. While important work was done by socially critical thinkers like the Russian Michael von Tugan-Baranowski,[14] the most significant and long-term research project was that initiated by an American student of Veblen's, Wesley C. Mitchell, at first independently, and then under the aegis of the National Bureau of Economic Research, founded in 1920. This empirical work produced genuine advances in the understanding of business ups and downs.

It became clear, for one thing, that the idea of a business cycle is a theoretical construction unifying a complex set of processes. Mitchell began the volume in which he presented the results of a statistical investigation into the cycle by observing that 'we have no statistical evidence of business cycles as whole. What the data show us are the fluctuations of particular processes . . .'. Thus the cycles 'turned out to be complexes, made up of divergent fluctuations in many processes'.[15] To say that 'the business cycle' is 'a synthetic product of the imagination',[16] however, is to accord it the same status as all scientific constructs. It is not to deny that it names something real, only to say that this reality, statistical in nature, is a matter of the interrelations between a large number of processes that produce the alternation of prosperity and depression experienced in the form of such phenomena as business slowdowns, unemployment and financial crises at some times, and as investment booms, increased trade, increased employment and financial opportunity at others.

Cycles and Profits

It was the large number of factors constituting business cycles that led to the competing explanations of the phenomenon, each taking one factor as primary. One of Mitchell's great contributions was his emphasis on the fact that what links these processes together is the practice that gives the modern social production system a unified history: the buying and selling of goods for money. Businesses buy goods from other businesses and labour from workers, who buy goods from businesses; these exchanges take the form of flows of money between businesses, individuals and banks or other financial institutions. Crises involve breakdowns in these flows, as bills can't be paid and investments, wage-payments and purchases are cut; the return of prosperity involves an expanded flow of money through the economy as new investments are made and workers are rehired. This is why, Mitchell observed, it 'is not until the uses of money have reached an advanced stage in a country that its economic vicissitudes take on the character of business cycles'.[17]

What makes money so central to modern society is that most goods and services are produced by businesses, and businesses are primarily engaged in the effort to make money. That is what business is about: using money to make money. The name for the money made by business is 'profit', the difference (in Mitchell's definition of a commonplace concept) 'between the prices which an enterprise pays for all the things it must buy, and the prices which the enterprise receives for all the things it sells'. Since a business enterprise must regularly turn a profit to continue to prosper, 'the making of profits is of necessity the controlling aim of business management', and decisions about where to invest and so what to produce are regulated by the quest for profit. Thus, as Mitchell put it: 'In business the useful goods produced by an enterprise are not the ends of endeavor, but the means toward earning profits.'[18] A company that does not turn a profit will soon go out of business; goods that cannot be sold at a profit will not be produced. Hence, most generally, 'Economic activity in a money-making world . . . depends upon the factors which affect present or prospective profits.'[19]

Investment decisions are not just a matter of the expectations stressed by economic theory, but equally of the actual ability to invest, since the money available for investment is either drawn from existing profits or borrowed against future profits, which must then come into existence if loans are to be repaid and the process is to continue. At some times businesses do better across the economy as a whole, earning more profit, on average, than at other times. When average profits are high society enjoys prosperity, but declining profits can lead to depression. All of this seems so obvious that what is surprising is the inability of most economists to grasp the mechanics of the process. With the advantage of a concentration on empirical studies of business conditions, together with his basic understanding of capitalism as a system centred on the production of money profits, Mitchell was led by his researches to the same conclusion as Haberler, that depressions are due to 'the absence of a sufficient margin between price and cost', that is, to insufficient profitability, while the opposite condition produces prosperity.

The absence of discussion of profitability as determining the state of the economy is as striking a feature of current economic writing, outside of a handful of left-wing outsiders, as the refusal to recognize the earlier history of depressions. This is probably due to the central place of the concept of 'national income' in macroeconomic theorizing (theorizing about the economy as a whole). The concept of 'growth', for instance, so central to contemporary economic discourse, is conventionally variously defined in terms of 'national income', defined as the market value of all goods and services produced in a country in a given year (GDP), as the total income earned by the sale of those goods and services or as the total amount spent on purchasing these goods and services (these three money totals are assumed to be equivalent).[20] In this total the profits of businesses enter as one sort of price or income alongside others, and thus only as a constituent of, rather than the chief determinant of, the overall state of the economy. In a society whose system of production and consumption is dominated by business, itself dominated by the need to earn a profit, growth – expansion of the system – is, as we have seen, a function of profitability. The national-income point of view, however, focuses on the overall change in income (or product value) produced by changes in profitability, so that consumer spending and investment in means of production seem to be independent contributors to economic growth.

In this, contemporary theorizing follows the founding example of Keynes himself. This is not surprising, as Keynes was the modern re-inventor of what is now called macroeconomics,[21] and the modern system of income accounts was devised to aid in Keynes-inspired policy-making. Since he was, after all, theorizing about capitalism, Keynes began *The General Theory* with a discussion of profit, also denoted 'entrepreneur's income', understood as what a businessman 'endeavours to maximize when he is deciding what amount of employment to offer'. But Keynes put theoretical stress on what he called 'the *total income* resulting from the employment given by the entrepreneur', consisting of profit plus factor cost (i.e. the prices of means of production and labour).[22] This was in order to move, a page or so later, to his central interest, the relation of the level of investment, and so of employment, to consumption and savings as fractions of the 'aggregate real income' of 'the community' as a whole.[23]

In this way, as Philip Mirowski points out, 'the national-income concept was effectively severed from capital, permitting the rate of increase of income to be analytically divorced from the rate of profit on capital'[24] (the latter – in Keynes's terminology, the 'marginal efficiency of capital' – now figures as one of the determinants of investment and so of national income). This is because Keynes, although he did not accept the neoclassical economists' doctrine that economic crisis was impossible, shared with them the basic idea that the economy is essentially a vast mechanism for allocating resources to satisfy consumption needs. On this assumption, the market's allocation of part of society's product to entrepreneurs as profit is just a way to get them to invest, in the interests of society as a whole. If the level of profitability is insufficient, Keynes reasoned, increasing employment and consumption by other means, specifically by government deficit spending, will lead to prosperity and continued growth.

Interestingly, as Mirowski has also noted, Keynes's use of the national income concept seems to have been indebted to W. C. Mitchell's work at the NBER, whose first research report was a statistical estimate of this quantity for the US. And in fact already in his 1927 study of business cycles, Mitchell moved from an emphasis on profitability as the key to cyclical phenomena, through the description of profits as 'the most variable type of income', to the complex flow of money payments throughout the economy as a whole, which makes profits 'subject to perturbations from a multitude of unpredictable causes'.[25] Although he emphasized profits as the factor dominating capitalist dynamics, Mitchell had no theoretical explanation for the vagaries of profitability. Thus he was finally left with no more to say than that 'defects in the system of guiding economic activity [by market-price relations] and the bewildering complexity of the task itself allow the processes of economic life to fall into those recurrent disorders which constitute crises and depressions.'[26]

An apparent counter-example to the neglect of profitability in contemporary business-cycle theorizing can be found in the views of the post-Keynesian economist Hyman P. Minsky, who argued like Mitchell that the 'validation of business debt', which makes possible continued financing and so ongoing economic activity, 'requires that prices and outputs be such that almost all firms earn large enough surpluses over labor and material costs' – profits, in other words – 'either to fulfill the gross payments required by debt or to induce refinancing'. Profits, in turn, are in his view determined by the scale of investment, which sets the demand for output and so makes possible (the realization of this possibility is simply assumed, without explanation) the appearance of a surplus above costs. And for Minsky, as for Keynes, investment is determined by 'the subjective nature of expectations about the future course of investment, as well as the subjective determination by bankers and their business clients of the appropriate liability structure for the financing of positions in different types of capital assets'.[27] Thus the rate of profit, a determinant of investors' expectations, is itself explained as a product of the expectation-driven behaviour of entrepreneurs and bankers.

Recent research into the American economy has confirmed Mitchell's common-sense focus on profits as central to the explanation of business fluctuations. As one important survey of American statistical material, carried out by economists whom no one could accuse of political radicalism, concluded, 'The effects of profit . . . dominate investment movements.'[28] And since investment determines the amount of money available to hire workers (and so for workers to spend on consumer goods) and to buy raw materials and plant and equipment, the growth or decline in investment affects the growth or decline of the economy as a whole. This explains why, as a recent study noted, profits stagnated or even began to decline several quarters before each of the three recessions, starting respectively in 1990, 2001 and 2007. Profit data going back to the last decades of the nineteenth century, when they were first collected, shows that something similar occurred in each of the recessions that the US economy has gone through since that time.[29]

Hence we are left with these basic questions: why do profits fall in the course of business expansions, and rise in the course of depressions? If profit is the difference between costs and sale prices, both measured in money, what determines the size of this difference? Since changes in the production and consumption of goods and services seem to be determined by relations between the money prices of these goods and services, what regulates these relations? These questions lead to the fundamental question: what is money, anyway, in a modern economy, such that business success or failure is determined by monetary gain or loss? These are questions that even a historically oriented economist like Mitchell did not think to ask, because he took for granted the existence of money as a means for coordinating social production and distribution activities. Asking them, for an inhabitant of capitalist society, would be like an ancient Egyptian asking why Osiris was in control of the Nile's ebb and flow and so of the rise and fall of agricultural output. Answering them requires sufficient intellectual distance from the conventions of our own society to step outside of everyday economic thinking and the theoretical elaborations of it formulated by economists, to consider money (and so profit) as historically peculiar social institutions, with particular consequences for the way we live.

3

Money, Profit and Cycles

What, actually, is money? The Wikipedia entry is an adequate representation of standard answers to this question: 'Money is anything that is generally accepted as payment for goods and services and repayment of debts.' The problem, of course, is that 'payment' means 'giving money in exchange for something'.[1] The circularity of the definition is no doubt unnoticed in large part just because, as Mitchell emphasized, in a modern business economy, 'most . . . economic activities have taken on the form of making and spending money'.

We are so used to this state of affairs that we hardly notice its historical peculiarity and forget that in the past – in much of the world, even the very recent past – most people made little or no use of money, since they produced much or most of their own food, clothing and other necessities of life. So it is worthwhile remembering that while money appears in many types of society, capitalism is the only one in which it plays such a central role in the production and distribution of goods and services that nearly every object and service that we make use of in the course of a day has to be purchased for money. In such a system, money has a different social significance from that of earlier societies.

Already in 1776 Adam Smith described capitalism as a system in which production processes are so complexly interrelated that each person is dependent on great numbers of others for his or her existence:

Observe the accommodation of the most common arti-
ficer or day-labourer in a civilized and thriving country,
and you will perceive that the number of people of
whose industry a part, though but a small part, has
been employed in producing him this accommodation,
exceeds all computation. The woolen coat, for example,
which covers the day-labourer, as coarse and rough as
it may appear, is the produce of the joint labour of a
great multitude of workmen. The shepherd, the sorter
of the wool, the wool-comber or carder, the dyer, the
scribbler, the spinner, the weaver, the fuller, the dresser,
with many others, must all join their different arts . . .
How many ship-builders, sailors, sail-makers, rope-
makers, must have been employed in order to bring
together the different drugs used by the dyer, which
often come from the remotest corners of the world.[2]

In a society in which most productive enterprises are
organized on a business basis, the normal functioning of
such a system of interdependent individuals depends on
the regular exchange of goods for money. This is because the
people who produce goods for a business have no direct
relationship with the people who will consume those goods
or services, even though it is ultimately for them that they
are producing. The workers in bakeries and automobile
factories do not know who will use the bread and the cars
they make, or what quantities they want and can afford. The
same is true of their employers. Each business only finds
out from its success or failure in selling its products, at sufficiently high prices to make a profit, to what extent it is meeting the needs of customers. Just because capitalist businesses
produce to meet the needs of anyone who can pay, as the
property of individuals or corporations they are linked to
the rest of society only as they buy materials and labour
and sell their products.

In talking about all societies we can speak abstractly of 'social productive activity', for in all social systems work must be done to transform natural resources into forms consumable by human beings. In every society, productive activity must be allocated among the different specific kinds of work necessary to produce the particular things and services that society wants to have available. In capitalism, a society in which most production is carried out by businesses, this allocation is carried out by finding out what quantities of what goods can be sold, rather than by some social process of deciding in what kinds of production to engage. Hence in capitalism the abstraction 'productive activity' is not only a matter of descriptive vocabulary but has acquired a physical form in money: it is the money received for a successfully marketed good that signifies that the labour that produced the good is part of social labour. The inter-relations between businesses and individuals constituting the economic system and so allocating its members' productive capacities are established by the use of this symbol. The exchange of goods for money, by thus making them inter-changeable with each other, erases the differences between the kinds of work necessary to produce them. Baking bread and assembling automobiles are equally represented by sums of money, the amounts paid for their respective products. It is by being exchanged for, and so treated as equal to, a sum of money (its price) that a good or service acquires economic reality – can actually be consumed – in this social system and that the effort made to produce it is counted as a contri-bution to economic life. Money thus represents the social character of the effort made to produce a good or service.

In modern society, based on the principle of individual ownership (even though the vast majority of people don't own very much), money represents the social character of productive activity in a form – bits of metal, paper symbols or electronic pulses – possessable by individuals. Business owners, like everyone else, have access to goods only in exchange for money; as Smith put it, 'It is not from the benevolence of the butcher, the brewer, or the baker, that we expect our dinner, but from their regard to their own interest.'[3] The particular product a business sells is of interest to it only as a means to acquire property that in the form of money can be exchanged for any sort of thing. Hence the use of money as a symbol for successfully social production does not simply facilitate the production, distribution and consumption of goods and services; money itself is the primary goal of business activity.

As Thorstein Veblen explained in his *Theory of Business Enterprise*,

> The all-dominating issue in business is the question of gain and loss. Gain and loss is a question of accounting, and the accounts are kept in terms of the money unit, not in terms of livelihood, nor in terms of the serviceability of the goods, nor in terms of the mechanical efficiency of the industrial or commercial plant . . . The business man judges of events from the standpoint of ownership, and ownership runs in terms of money.[4]

Executives move capital from one area of business to another not because they care more about automobiles than soya beans or stuffed animals, but to make money.

Money is central to our social system because it is the first such system in which most productive activity – apart from the few tasks that people still perform for themselves, like (sometimes) cooking dinner, brushing their teeth or hobbies – is wage labour, performed in exchange for money. The situation is the reverse of that in the past: most people, lacking access to land, tools and raw materials, or enough money to purchase these, cannot produce the goods – housing, clothes, food – they need; and they must work for others who have the money to hire them as well as to supply materials and tools. This money flows back to the employers when employees purchase goods they – as a class – have produced. Meanwhile, employers buy and sell goods – raw materials, machinery, consumer goods – from and to each other.

Since it is by the exchange of products for money that the different kinds of work that make these products are recognized as the elements of a connected system, this practice provides the main form in which adjustments can be made among all the myriad processes that constitute the economy, thus allocating the total working ability of society to the different tasks whose output is desirable at any time. More highly skilled work, for instance, is acknowledged as more productive than less skilled work when the product of an hour of the former commands a higher price than the product of an hour of the latter. Most generally, the relations between market prices provide a (constantly changing and in any case always approximate) method of representing the interrelations between different labour processes. It provides a measure of the contribution of earlier production processes to current production, in the form of the prices of raw materials, buildings and tools. When goods are sold, the prices paid for them signal the extent to which social demand makes it worthwhile for businesses to expend resources in producing them. If those prices yield a profit, they will continue to be produced; otherwise, they will not be. Most radically, if goods aren't sold, the work done to produce them and that required earlier to produce the raw materials and machinery used might as well not have been done. In this case, from the business point of view, none of the work involved in producing the goods has even paid for itself, much less turned a profit.[5]

Profit

The profit that forms a portion of the sales price of goods and services is an essential part of the economic mechanism because the individuals or corporate entities that own businesses go through the trouble of organizing the production and distribution of goods and services in order to make money. (This much the conventional view gets right, of course; what it misses is that, as Mitchell emphasized, it is the making of money, not the production of goods, which is the goal of the process.) They require money to meet their own consumption needs, but also to meet the needs of business itself. Business expansion requires money for investment, and under competitive conditions, businesses that don't expand may not exist for long. Since no one will continue in a line of business that does not make a profit, the ability to make money – to increase the quantity owned of the representation of social productive activity – constrains what goods are produced, or even whether money is invested in the production of goods at all. In a continuous process, to quote Veblen again, 'investments are made for profit, and industrial plants and processes are capitalized [treated as worth particular sums of money] on the basis of their profit-yielding capacity'.[6]

It is with the goal of making money that employers buy equipment and materials from each other and labour from employees, who in turn buy back the portion of their product not used to replace or expand the productive apparatus and – let's not forget – to provide the employers with their own, generally expensive, consumables. (Thus part of profit takes such forms as dividends paid to investors and executive salaries.) The capitalistically desired output of this whole process, profit, is the money-representation of the labour performed beyond that required to reproduce the class of employees (paid in the form of wages) and to produce the goods required for production. Profit, as a portion of the sales price, misleadingly appears to be generated by the activities of particular firms because it is appropriated by individual businesses, who compete with each other to get as much of it as possible. In reality, profit only comes into practical existence as produced goods are exchanged for money; that is, as their particularity as products of particular firms disappears into their character as parts of the total social product. It is a portion of the total productive labour of society, as represented by the abstract money symbolism. Because profit is just what is left over after the funds required for production goods and labour have been reconstituted by the exchange of all goods produced against money, it is the social system that produces profit, though individual companies get to keep it.

As the illusion that companies individually produce the profit their owners receive illustrates, the fact that money is the most important practical way in which the social aspect of productive activity is represented allows it to misrepresent social reality as well. Since goods will only be produced if they can be sold at prices that allow businesses to make a profit, the amount something costs reflects what people are willing to pay rather than its actual place in the production system. As a result, the prices of individual goods may be higher or lower than what would be warranted by the time taken to produce them, though – since money's role is defined by the totality of exchanges – that means that some other goods will receive accordingly lower or higher prices than they should.[7] Some capitalists (merchants and other middlemen) specialize in the sale of goods and services produced by others; they therefore claim a portion of the profits that the latter would otherwise keep. It can seem, accordingly, that the process of selling itself generates profit. By being exchanged for money, natural resources like land and oil deposits are represented in the same terms – as worth sums of money – as humanly produced things. Interest – more money – must be paid for the use of someone else's money. So money itself seems to have a price. Similarly, things that are simply symbols of money, like IOUs, including complicated IOUs like bank-notes, stocks and bonds issued by companies, and even Collateralized Debt Obligations, can be bought and sold as if they were real commodities, since they entitle their owners to money incomes and so are treated as if they were saleable products. Thus portions of capitalist profit are diverted to owners of natural resources (as rent) and money (as interest), whose property seems to 'earn' these portions as a matter of course.[8] For this reason, any form of investment that claims a share of profit seems as much an 'industry' as the actual production of goods, and the earnings on these investments appear as, for instance, real-estate 'industry' and financial 'industry' profits. (As we will see later, taxes are another portion of profit which it is hard to recognize as such.)

The social-systemic character of profit can be seen in the very fact that the level of profitability on capital investment alters over time, independently of the wishes of businessmen, who, like everyone else, must adapt to the price movements that determine how well they do. (It is this that gives rise to the idea of 'the economy' as a set of impersonal forces like the laws of nature.[9]) Competition for profit forces businesses to charge similar prices for similar products; since they must themselves buy goods (labour and materials) which have costs fixed at any moment, their ability to compete by lowering prices depends on the production techniques they employ. If firms in a certain industry are able to limit competition by the formation of monopoly or near-monopoly situations, the extra profits they earn mean lower profits for firms in other industries. Under more and less competitive situations alike, therefore, the social character of the system asserts itself through pressure on firms to seek lower costs for raw materials, and other inputs to production, and to raise the productivity of labour, insofar as this leads to higher profits for individual firms.

Trends and Cycles

It is the nature of capitalist society, in which production is based on wage labour and so organized by the exchange of goods for money, that has led historically to a strong tendency towards decreasing the labour employed in comparison to the amount it produces (while, of course, increasing the number of workers absolutely as the system grew). By lowering costs per unit of product, this increased profitability. Employers first made labour more productive by assembling workers into large workshops, within which their work was divided into smaller and smaller tasks. This led to the substitution of machines for people, whenever this raised profitability, and eventually to the invention of the modern assembly line, whose speed enforced high levels of labour intensity. By the end of the twentieth century, most production had become mechanized mass production, requiring less and less labour relative to a growing quantity of machinery. In the United States, to take a nation with a particularly long series of statistical data, the monetary value of the stock of machinery and equipment per person employed grew by one calculation from $281,000 in 1830 to $39,636,000 in 1992, while investment in non-residential structures went from $3,503,000 to $72,625,000 (in 1990 international dollars). Similar numbers hold for France, Germany, the Netherlands, the UK and Japan (though only the latter reached US-level rates of investment by 1992).[10] And, of course, as increasing mechanization raises labour productivity, growing amounts of raw materials must be used (and paid for) per person, because more materials are required for growing amounts of product.

This shift has obvious consequences for the profitability of capital. Profit, as we saw, is the money-representation of the labour performed by employees of all of society's productive businesses in excess of the work required to replace raw materials, tools and those employees themselves. If those businesses increasingly invest more of their money in machines and materials than in labour, then the amount invested in the doing of work, and so able to generate profit in addition to reproducing the labour force, will decline relative to total investment. There will therefore be a tendency (offset by the lowering of labour costs and the cheapening of machinery and raw materials) for profitability to fall: a tendency Marx called 'the most important law of modern political economy'.[11] His explanation of the tendency to declining profits, hypothesized well before him by nineteenth-century economists, is a controversial one, to say the least. But it led Marx to an analysis of the cycle of depressions and prosperities that explains the intimate relationship Mitchell and others have observed to hold between the business cycle, changes in profitability and the centrality of money to the modern economy.

Marx argued that the growth of capitalism, with its bias towards mechanization, would led to an increase in the amount of money needed to continue to expand production, and so to a tendency for the size of individual companies to increase. This prediction is acknowledged by all observers to have been fulfilled. One consequence of this is that if the profitability of capital falls, at some point the amount of profit available will be inadequate for further expansion of the system as a whole, though individual firms may be able to continue growing. Slowing or stagnant investment means a shrinking market for produced goods. Employers neither invest capital in the purchase of buildings, machinery and raw materials nor pay the wages that workers would have spent on consumer goods. A slowdown in investment is experienced by workers as a rise in unemployment and by businessmen as a contraction of markets (and explained by Keynesian economists as a consequence of insufficient demand). This is a self-magnifying process, as declining demand causes business failures, higher unemployment and further contraction of demand. At the same time, since businessmen (and other borrowers) are increasingly unable to meet financial obligations, the various forms of IOUs issued by banks and brokerage houses become increasingly valueless, causing a financial crisis, while falling stock prices reflect the declining value of business enterprises. Individuals and institutions hoard money, rather than invest it. In short, capitalism finds itself in a depression.

But in a capitalist economy, what causes suffering for individuals can be good for the system. As firms go bankrupt and production goods of all sorts go unsold, the surviving companies can buy up buildings, machinery and raw materials at bargain prices, while land values fall. In this way the money-representation of goods produced at an earlier time is recalibrated at a lower level. There is also market pressure for the design of new, more efficient and cheaper machinery. As a result, the cost of capital investment declines. At the same time, rising unemployment drives down wages. Capitalists' costs are thus lower while the labour they employ is more productive than before, as people are made to work harder and on newer equipment. The result is a revival in the rate of profit, which makes possible a new round of investment and therefore an expansion of markets for production goods and consumer goods alike. A depression, that is, is the cure for insufficient profits; it is what makes the next period of prosperity possible, even as that prosperity will in turn generate the conditions for a new depression.

This is, of course, a highly abstract, schematic picture of developments that in each particular case present unique aspects and are complicated by historically specific phenomena. A depression may be initiated by a stock market crash, as in 1929, or by a banking crisis, as in 2007; the American depression of 1837 began with a collapse in inflated real-estate values. The last Great Depression led into a world war, which affected its history in unprecedented ways. But in all such cases, declining profitability, resulting from the decline in labour employed relative to capital investment as a whole, led to a slowdown or cessation of economic growth, which in turn produced the conditions for increased profitability and a new prosperity. Despite its abstraction, the picture sketched above provides a way to understand the pattern of boom and bust, and in particular its relation to the flow and ebb of business profits, which has marked the history of capitalism.

It will also help us understand the ways in which the pattern changed during the years after the Second World War. The idea of the business cycle was so well established, and the Great Depression of the 1930s so severe and so terrible in its ultimate political and social effects, that after the war fear of a new depression was only slowly displaced by the hope that Keynesian methods would be able to control the cycle. Neither the hope nor the fear was fulfilled: on the one hand, the business cycle did not end; on the other, despite recessions, debt crises, stock market crashes and other economic disasters, capitalism did not undergo a crisis and depression like those that plagued it from the nineteenth century to the 1930s – at least, until now. To understand how capitalism has altered since the war, and the consequences of this alteration for the current situation, we must review the history of the last 60 years.

4

After the Golden Age

While the coming of the Second World War had returned the United States to full employment, this was only by way of government deficit-financed spending for arms production, not because of the revival of the private-enterprise economy. Peace, with the decline in war work and the demobilization of millions of soldiers, brought a sharp decline in industrial production and a rise in unemployment; by 1946, however, a strong upward movement was clear. Capital expenditure, to replace and modernize industrial plant, rose from $7 to $20 billion between 1945 and 1948; there was also a significant increase in commercial, industrial and residential building. At the same time, the US became the world's leading exporter, both of goods and of investment capital, particularly to European countries.[1]

Europe, meanwhile, had ended the war in a state of ruin. Within a few years, however, the European economy was reviving: while in 1945 'industrial production was barely 40 percent of prewar levels in Belgium, France, and the Netherlands, and less than 20 percent in Germany and Italy', two years later it exceeded 1938 levels, except for western Germany, where the occupation forces still kept efforts to restart industry in check.[2] With the start of the Cold War and America's desire for 'a vibrant and prosperous European economy to provide a bulwark against the Soviet Union',[3] Germany was not only allowed but vigorously aided, notably by the Marshall Plan, to retake its place as the economic centre of Europe. Recovery throughout Europe 'was driven by spending on industrial capacity', with priority given to heavy industry. Meanwhile, 'trade unionists and the left, extending even to Communist Party hardliners, approached postwar reconstruction as a national effort comparable to the resistance', keeping wages low and working conditions hard.[4] In Japan, also seriously damaged physically and economically by the war, American aid played an important role in powering the post-war revival, especially with the coming of the Korean War.[5] Here too wage restraint and industrial investment were key factors in the rapid production of a 'miracle economy'.

Thus, despite the particular features of the Great Depression, most importantly the war into which it opened, the post-1945 revival of the capitalist economy followed, in broad outline, the pattern set in previous episodes of economic collapse and regeneration – the pattern to be expected in a society regulated by money profit. The depression had been long-lasting and the level of physical and economic destruction of capital unusually high; it is not surprising therefore that the revival led to an exceptionally long prosperity. In Angus Madisson's words, 'The years 1950 to 1973 were a "golden age"', which saw 'a growth of GDP and GDP per capita on an unprecedented scale in all parts of the world economy, a rapid growth of world trade, a reopening of world capital markets and possibilities for international [labour] migration'.[6] This is not an idiosyncratic view: all commentators agree on describing this period as an unusually prosperous period for capitalism.

The exceptional length of the Golden Age, which, as a historian of the American economy put it, 'went on steadily through mild recessions instead of exhausting itself after a few years',[7] was due also to the continuation into the post-depression period of what had by then come to be called Keynesian methods. If capitalism remained at base the same system, the economic policy practiced by governments had changed. On the one hand, the political dangers threatened by the social movements unleashed by the Great Depression, when mass unemployment radicalized the population, were unacceptable to the governing elite of the capitalist states, especially in the context of what was believed to be an epic confrontation with Communism.[8] On the other hand, it was also imagined that Keynesian methods of deficit financing could definitively control the ravages of the business cycle, moderating economic declines until the tendency towards growth supposedly natural to the economy could reassert itself.

As a result, Maddison observes, a 'major feature of the golden age was the substantial growth in the ratio of governmental spending to GDP', which 'rose from 27 per cent of GDP in OECD countries in 1950 to 37 per cent in 1973'.[9] In most countries this was due largely to increases in welfare-state spending on such matters as social security, education and healthcare. In the United States it included sizeable sums spent on war and preparations for war. In the words of economist Philip A. Klein, writing for the conservative American Enterprise Institute, 'America's "longest peacetime expansion" – from 1961 to 1969 – was influenced greatly by the redefinition of the term "peacetime" to include the Vietnam War and the increase in defense spending from $50 billion in fiscal year 1965 to $80 billion in fiscal year 1968 . . .'.[10] This American expansion in turn helped power global growth, notably by way of the revival of Japan and the take-off of Korea, particularly stimulated in the Vietnam War period.

In other words, the capitalist economy proper – the private enterprise system – was, even after the profit-restoring effects of a depression lasting from 1929 to 1945, not by itself able to produce a level of well-being sufficient, in the eyes of social decision-makers, to achieve a politically desirable level of social contentment. Thus, for example, when a

Republican government, acting on its anti-New Deal, pro-free enterprise ideology, cut defence spending after the end of the Korean War in 1953 without adding offsetting increases in domestic expenditure, the United States experienced a sharp drop in production and a correspondingly sharp increase in unemployment. Despite its wishes, the Eisenhower administration quickly acted to lower interest rates and increase government spending, including on public works as well as on directly military projects.[11] In the United States, in fact, political economist Joyce Kolko noted in 1988, 'roughly half of all new employment after 1950 was created by state expenditures, and a comparable shift occurred in the other OECD nations'.[12] In this way, post-war government spending on military and civilian projects increased the demand for goods and services, creating prosperous conditions despite the limitations of the capitalist economy.

Keynes's idea had been that the government would borrow money in times of depression to get the economy moving again; when national income expanded in response, it could then be harmlessly taxed to pay back the debt. In reality, crisis management turned into a permanent state-private 'mixed economy'. After the mid-1970s, throughout the capitalistically developed countries, national debt, far from being repaid, grew, both absolutely and in relation to GDP. This growing debt made itself felt in a tendency towards inflation, as businesses increased prices (and workers tried to catch up) to offset the rising chunk of national income taken by government. In particular, the inflation stimulated as the US Treasury printed dollars required for the debt-financing of American government operations spread through the world, given the post-war role of the dollar as a global reserve currency.

Under the post-war arrangement entered into by the world's capitalist nations (the Bretton Woods system), the dollar, representing a fixed amount of gold, served as a standard against which the value of other currencies could be measured, thus facilitating international trade and investment. By 1971, so many dollars had been created to pay for American wars and domestic programmes that the US had to sever the dollar's tie with gold to avoid the possibility that Fort Knox might be emptied as other nations cashed in their greenbacks. Despite the opinion of many, this did not basically alter the nature of money, which had long functioned largely on the basis of credit and state fiat money. But it did signal how far the world economy had moved from the self-regulating mechanism imagined by free-market enthusiasts towards a system dependent on constant management by governmental authorities – and one in which the relaxation of management, or the limitations on its reach, would make way for dire developments.

In fact, despite the panoply of governmental interventions and 'automatic stabilizers' set in place to keep the economy on an even keel, the Golden Age came to an end in the early 1970s. World growth slowed dramatically, with declining rates of investment and productivity and increasing unemployment. At the time this recession was commonly blamed on the 'shock' of a rapid rise in oil prices, engineered by the OPEC countries in collusion with oil companies, in an effort to increase their share of the world's profits and to offset the fall in the value of the dollar, the currency in which oil prices are set. But the fact that growth on the earlier scale did not resume when the world economy adjusted to this change, and even when oil prices declined again, indicates that some more fundamental alteration in the global economy was underway.

Warning signs had been visible for a while. As economist William Nordhaus observed in an article published by the Brookings Institution in 1974, 'by most reckonings [US] corporate profits have taken a dive since 1966', even taking into account the record profits of the oil companies in 1973. 'The poor performance of corporate profits is not limited to the United States', he continued. 'A secular decline in the share of profits has also occurred in most of Western Europe.'[13] Once again a boom, with its attendant increase, relative to labour, in capital invested in means of production had led to declining profits and so to an end of prosperity – although the turning point to which this process led by 1974 once again took on a hitherto unknown form.

It is not surprising, in view of the history of the business cycle, that the post-war period of prosperity came to an end in the 1960s. But the end of the Golden Age did not lead, as some at the time feared it would, to a crisis and depression of the traditional sort, just as the level of social wellbeing had been maintained after the war despite the limitation of economic growth. In Europe, 'public expenditure rose from 38 percent of [GDP] in 1967–69 to 46 percent in 1974–76', with spending, above all on transfer payments and social programmes, 'especially rapid in Germany, the Netherlands, Denmark, and Sweden'.[14] In Japan, government spending rose from 19.3 per cent of GDP in 1970 to 27.3 per cent in 1975 and 32.2 per cent in 1980. In the United States, where the index of industrial production dropped at a 24.8 per cent annual rate between September 1974 and March 1975, while employment fell at a 6.7 per cent annual rate, a major depression was averted by a massive increase in government spending, from $264.8 billion in 1973 to $356.9 billion in 1975 (it had been $40.8 billion in 1950). Between government purchases of goods and services, both civilian and military, and transfer payments to households, the effect was a rapid infusion of cash into the economy that showed up in household consumption and in 'a rise in corporate cash flows'.[15] At the same time, the financial aspect of the crisis – the 1974 failure of the multi-billion dollar Franklin National Bank and the serious difficulty of other banks – were contained by the actions of the Federal Reserve and other government institutions acting as lenders of last resort.

Instead of a new depression, therefore, the world's capitalist economies experienced a short, though serious, recession. But, confirming the idea that depressions are the cure for the insufficient profitability that produces them, the use of government funds to limit the extent of the downturn meant that the following prosperous period was also limited. In Tom Kemp's description,

> The clearing of ground for recovery by a downward revaluation of assets and the lowering of costs, thus restoring the profitability of capital, did not happen in the classic manner. What did happen . . . was that plants that proved unprofitable in the recession [of 1974–5] did not reopen in the boom; 'de-industrialization' had begun.[16]

Government spending reappeared as corporate profits, as well as in the form of income (transfer payments), to be spent on goods and services produced by private businesses. But these profits – matched in national balance sheets by surging government debt and fiscal deficits – were not produced in the private sector (the capitalist economy proper), from which in fact they were taken in the form of taxes and loans. Since the earlier decline in profit rates had been counteracted rather than overcome, it is not surprising that corporations used the funds available to them less for building new factories to produce more goods than for squeezing more profit out of existing production by investing in labour- and energy-saving equipment while labour costs were lowered by moving plants from high-wage to low-wage areas or simply by using the threat of such moves to cut wages and benefits. (The results of this included a lasting increase in unemployment in Western Europe and in what became the Rust Belt of the US.)

Of course, the widely observed workplace speed-up, dismantling of occupational safety measures and extension of the work week, along with increasing employment of part-time and temporary workers, also helped lower the average wage and so increase profitability. Between 1970 and 1985, average annual wage growth in the United States declined from more than 12 per cent to around 4 per cent. Between wage stagnation and inflation average weekly earnings declined by 14.3 per cent between 1970 and 1986, while median household income dipped by about 6 per cent between 1973 and 1986;[17] household incomes were maintained to the extent they were only by the massive entrance of married women into the labour force. Especially in the US, the steadily increasing facilitation of consumer debt – from credit-card financing to easy-to-get mortgages – that helped maintain the level of business activity was also another means, like inflation, to lower wages by raising prices: the additional cost of items is collected by financial institutions under the name of interest. Pension plans made part of workers' earnings available for use by brokerage firms, banks and other financial institutions; in the United States, their replacement by the personal stock-investment plans called 401(k)s, like the weakening or elimination of job-linked healthcare plans, further diminished labour costs.

Starting in the 1980s, spending on the socialized wage payments constituted by welfare-state programmes was cut in all countries, to different extents depending on local political conditions, freeing up money for corporate use. The restructuring of tax laws to transfer income from workers to high-income recipients, practiced most extravagantly in the United States,[18] cut wages directly, in a decades-long process theoretically justified by the 'supply side' theory that capitalists' mere possession of increased amounts of money will lead to its investment, however low profit expectations may be. In reality none of this, given the high level of existing investment in means of production relative to labour costs, was enough to restore a high level of profitability. As a result, in the words of a recent survey of the period,

> Between 1973 and the present, economic performance in the US, western Europe, and Japan has, by every standard macroeconomic indicator, deteriorated, business cycle by business cycle, decade by decade (with the exception of the second half of the 1990s). Equally telling, over the same period, capital investment on a world scale, and in every region besides China, even including the east Asian [Newly Industrializing Countries] since the middle 1990s, has grown steadily weaker.[19]

The slowdown in productive investment meant that money was increasingly available for other purposes. Corporations began to spend vast sums they might earlier have used to expand production to buy up and reconfigure existing companies, selling off parts of them for quick profits and manipulating share prices to make money on the stock market. In the late 1980s, it has been calculated, about 70 per cent of the rise in the Standard & Poor's index of American stock values was due to the effects of takeovers and buyouts;[20] over the next twenty years the excess of stock prices over the underlying values of the companies they represent continued to grow. Thus the merger and acquisitions boom of the 1980s shaded into a larger pattern of speculating in financial markets rather than investing in productive enterprises. To take just one area of speculation, the value of funds involved in currency trading – buying and selling different national moneys to take advantage of small shifts in exchange rates – rose from $20 billion in 1973 to $1.25 trillion in 2000, an increase far greater than the growth in trade of actual goods and services.

Avenues for speculation were multiplied by the invention of new 'financial instruments', such as derivatives, swaps and the now infamous 'securitization' of various forms of debt, including home mortgages. (For an idea of how far the imaginative mirroring of actual invested money by the creation of new saleable claims to it went, consider the fact that by the time of the crisis of mid-September 2007 the world's estimated $167 trillion in financial assets had given rise to $596 trillion in derivatives, basically bets on the future movements of asset prices.)

This 'massive shift toward speculative uses of liquidity . . . expressed itself in a strong push to legislative deregulation . . .'.[21] Deregulation, that is, was a response to the pressure to speculate; though of course it made risk-taking easier; it was not the cause of increased speculation. Similarly, to explain the rise of debt-financed acquisitions and other modes of speculation as the effect of greed, as is often done today, is doubly silly: not only does it leave unexplained the sudden increase of greediness in recent decades, but it also ignores the basic motive of capitalist investment decisions, which must always be guided by the expected maximum profits achievable in a reasonably short term. Similarly to the way that playing the lottery, despite its multimillion-to-one odds, represents the most probable path to wealth for the average worker, speculation simply came to offer businesspeople better chances for higher profits than productive investment.

Along with speculation, the low level of profitability led to steady growth of corporate debt, especially as the inflationary response to government spending encouraged borrowing, since the falling value of money lowered interest costs. In the United States, companies had traditionally financed expansion out of their own profits, but in 1973 corporate borrowing exceeded internal financing and this was only the beginning. (Around the same time France saw a US-style move to borrowing, the traditional mode of corporate financing in Germany.) The increasing uncertainty of economic affairs led in particular to a growth in short-term debt, though this in itself helped produce a rising rate of corporate bankruptcies, as sudden fluctuations of fortune could make it impossible to repay loans in short order.

To a large extent, especially since the 1980s, the 'globalization' of capital is part of this pattern of growth in speculation and debt. The last quarter-century has certainly seen a worldwide expansion of production and trade and the relocation of some production operations to a few low-wage areas.[22] But, like domestic investment, the export of capital – which in any case has remained overwhelmingly within the capitalistically developed economies of the OECD – has been largely driven, in the words of Paolo Giussani, 'by sectors more or less directly tied to finance and short-term speculation'.[23] As a recent OECD study reports, foreign direct investment (FDI) became 'increasingly dominated by service industries and mergers and acquisitions (M&AS)', so that 'manufacturing's share of global FDI inflows fell from 41% in 1990 to approximately 30% in 2005', and by 2006 M&AS 'accounted for two-thirds of all FDI inflows, although these levels were slightly below the record levels of 2000'.[24]

Between 1971 and 1976 the number of international branches of the world's 50 largest banks grew by more than 60 per cent. American banks in particular increased their global presence; the foreign share of Citicorp's banking activity, for example, expanded from 40 to 70 per cent. 'In this way a gigantic financial structure emerged, free of control by central banks and from the costs of reserve requirements, with an autonomous capacity to increase liquidity.'[25] Dollars poured into this structure when the US balance of payments became increasingly negative as the American government made use of the reserve-currency character of the dollar to pay for its increasing expenses and 'petro-dollars' accumulated in OPEC countries. But already by 1980, when world dollar deposits were less than $50 billion, bank-generated credits (that is, money lent on the assumption it will be repaid before the bank has to meet its own liabilities) surpassed $223 billion.

The 1970s had seen rapid growth in lending to under-developed countries, as commercial banks replaced govern-mental and international agencies as the main sources of borrowed money. Between 1975 and 1982, notably, Latin American debt to commercial banks grew at a rate of over 20 per cent a year. Debt service grew even faster, as refinanc-ing piled interest charges on interest charges. The result was a series of debt crises that wracked Latin America after the early 1980s. One consequence was the abandonment of inter-nal economic development projects in these countries in favour of the export-oriented economic strategies demanded by the international economic authorities (the World Bank and International Monetary Fund) that oversaw the restruc-turing of debt. A similar fate was in store for loans advanced to the centrally planned economies of Eastern Europe. Their disastrous entanglement in debt, which seemed originally to provide a way out of the declining fortunes of the state-run systems, was an important step towards the integration of the former 'communist' world into the global capitalist system. (I remember, fifteen years ago, suggesting to a Hun-garian dissident, György Konrád, who had just finished extolling integration into the world market as a solution for his country's problems, that the East might be joining the West just as the capitalist economy's happy days were over; he replied that he had finally met in me someone more pessimistic than a Hungarian.) By 1984, America joined this club, taking in more foreign investment than it exported, and a year later the US became a net debtor. It gradually turned into the world's largest recipient of investment and the world's largest debtor, seriously dependent on foreign lending to finance both its wars and its unhinged consumption of much of the world's production.

In all these ways, then, debt – promises to pay sometime in the future – took the place of the money the slowing capitalist economy failed to generate. Since governments, businesses and, to an ever-increasing degree, individuals used borrowed funds to purchase goods and services, public, corporate and household debt appeared on bank and other business balance sheets as profits. Such a state of affairs is necessarily unstable, open to disruption by forces ranging from the speculative activities of individuals, as when George Soros forced a devaluation of the British pound in 1992 (earning an estimated $1.1 billion in the process), to the decisions of scores of businesses to move money in and out of national and regional economies, as when the weakening of the Thai real estate market in 1997 led to the collapse of the Thai currency, the baht, and then to credit crises in places as distant as Brazil and Russia. The worldwide stock market crash of October 1987 produced the largest vaporization of virtual values in United States history, reminding observers of the Wall Street crash of 1929 and prefiguring the meltdown of 2008.

The maintenance of low interest rates by the Federal Reserve enabled the rise and fall of the dot-com bubble in the US between 1995 and 2001, as investors financed internet-based companies that were supposed to ride the crest of a new, information technology-enhanced economy. A similar frenzy developed in Europe with the debt-based development of mobile phone networks in Germany, Italy and the United Kingdom. The crash of stock-market values sent $5 trillion of investors' money up in smoke between March 2000 and October 2002. Seeking new avenues for speculation, investors turned to the housing market; as economist Robert Schiller noted already in 2005: 'Once stocks fell, real estate became the primary outlet for the speculative frenzy that the stock market had unleashed. Where else could plungers apply their newly acquired trading talents?'[26]

Throughout the 1990s, the deeper reality at the bottom of the wild swings of speculative fortune – the insufficient profits earned by money invested in production, relative to the level of economic growth required to incorporate the world's population into a prosperous capitalism – showed itself in such phenomena as the depression, born of the fizzling of a real-estate bubble, that has afflicted Japan since 1990; the continuing high unemployment in relatively prosperous Europe; the stagnation of the American economy, with falling wages, rising poverty levels and dependence on constantly increasing debt – personal, corporate and national – to maintain even a simulacrum of the fabled 'American standard of living'; the continual slipping back into economic difficulties of the nations of Latin America, despite periodic (though uneven) successes in mastering them; the relegation of most of Africa, despite its vast natural resources, to unrelenting misery except for the handful of rulers salting away the proceeds from oil and mineral sales in Swiss banks; the analogous limitation of Russian capitalism to the machinations of former party apparatchiks-turned-millionaires; and the historically unprecedented accumulation of hundreds of millions of un- or under-employed people in gigantic slums around the world. This is the reality that has persisted beneath the alternating contractions and expansions, the debt crises and their temporary resolutions, the currency collapses and financial panics that have shuttled from one part of the world to another over the last 30 years.

The result was the economic situation that arrived so shockingly in 2007, though for several decades the warning signs – debt crises, recessions, bank collapses, stock market failures – were clear enough. Generally ascribed to lax regulation, greed or bad central-bank policy, the current economic collapse is in line with the whole history of capitalism as a system. What we are faced with today is a further, more serious manifestation of the depression that first announced itself dramatically in the mid-1970s, but which governmental economic policy was able hold at bay – in part by displacing it to poor parts of the world, but largely by a historically unprecedented creation of public, private and individual debt, in the rich parts – for 30-odd years. Perhaps its full force can be further delayed with additional infusions of credit. It is also possible that the ongoing unravelling of the world economy, most visible at the moment in such different areas as Greece, Ireland, Britain and Japan, will continue, with more dire consequences than we have yet seen. What can – and cannot – be done?

5

Appropriate Policies

On 1 March 2009 the *New York Times* 'News of the Week in Review' included a page of opinions from noted economists on the prospects for the economy, given the ongoing crisis and the various attempts – Troubled Assets Relief Program, bailouts, stimulus, budget plan – made so far to deal with it. Most more or less shared the forecast of Professor Nouriel Roubini of New York University, that the recession would not end until some time in 2011. The most optimistic (like Federal Reserve Bank chairman Ben Bernanke himself a few days earlier) thought that it would all be over in a year, while financier and author George Cooper saw a possible 'two or more decades of readjustment'. Most were careful to hedge their bets by adding a proviso that a near-term recovery could be expected only if (to use Roubini's phrasing) 'appropriate policies' were 'put in place'. Not specifying what those policies were, of course, only strengthened the prediction safety factor. But then no one based his or her predictions on any serious analysis of the nature and causes of the crisis or the efficacy of the various remedies.[1]

In fact, it's hard to imagine a more stunning demonstration of the theoretical bankruptcy of economics as a putative science than the ongoing discussion of the Great Recession. Just as no deeper explanation has been offered for 2007's catastrophic events than that they were the fallout from a credit crisis caused by excessive debt peddled by and to financial institutions around the world, no cure has been proposed for what is commonly described as an illness gripping the economy other than the standard 'Keynesian' and 'neoliberal' remedies: the first calls for some combination, in different amounts, of the continued intravenous feeding of the financial system with government money, along with subsidization of selected industries, modest amounts of public works spending, extended unemployment benefits, increasing access to minimal health insurance and greater regulation of the banking industry to prevent a repeat performance. The second, as in the contribution to the *Times* symposium by William Poole of the ultra-conservative Cato Institute (and former St Louis Reserve Bank president) is simply to wait for 'the self-correcting nature of markets' to kick in. In fact, according to Poole, 'Federal policy is damaging the economy' since its stimulative effects will be 'offset by anticipated higher taxes and the need to finance the deficit', which will inhibit investment.

The dispute among pundits is matched by real-world conflicts among politicians, businessmen and economic officials over how to react to the ongoing weakness of the economy.[2] While the United States undertook to spend 4.8 per cent of its expected GDP by 2010, and China planned a 6 per cent of GPD stimulus over the next two years – sums that a 2009 editorial in the *Times*, a far from extremist newspaper, pronounced 'still too small' – European governments did not come near to this level of spending. The struggles in spring 2010 over bailing out the collapsing Greek economy – necessary to safeguard other national bank and private holdings of Greek bonds, to attempt to block the spread of the Greek disaster to other, larger European economies and to preserve the euro as a continent-wide currency – provided a vivid illustration of the European hesitation over expansive government action. Even when European finance ministers were finally compelled to offer their weakest partners a rescue package of nearly $1 trillion, with backup from the IMF, 'some bankers questioned whether [this] would be enough to calm the markets over the long term. One banker said that, with more European economies coping with rising deficits, raising, guaranteeing or backing such a large sum would not be an easy task.' Said one expert, David Marsh, speaking of the richest European nation: 'I don't think that there is enough commitment or economic firepower in Germany to provide the massive loan guarantees to satisfy the markets.'[3] The fund responsible for rescue itself, in fact, when invented was 'more a theoretical construct' than an actual programme: it institutionalized a commitment made to lend money in the future 'if a large economy like Spain, which represents 12 percent of the output of the euro zone, asks for assistance'.[4]

Finding the European hesitation over recession-fighting spending 'especially puzzling', Obama economic adviser Christina Romer asserted that the New Deal response to the depression of the 1930s had shown that 'fiscal stimulus works'.[5] If the lesson of history is this clear, the European response is indeed puzzling, as is the modest scale of the American stimulus, decried by forthright Keynesians like Paul Krugman. But, of course, history's lessons are not univocal. One can, for instance, argue that history demonstrates the failure of the New Deal to end the Great Depression.[6] It is true that by 1935 the panoply of measures set in motion by the Roosevelt administration – banking subsidies and regulation, industrial price controls, subsidization of agribusiness, unemployment and old-age insurance, federal make-work programmes and support for unionization – had helped arrest the downward trend that began in the late 1920s. Yet two years later, when the Roosevelt government cut spending sharply, investment and production fell again, unemployment increased (there were ten million unemployed by 1938) and at best stagnation seemed to be the order of the day. Only with the coming of the Second World War, and the dedication of resources to preparing for war, did 'fiscal stimulus' finally produce something like full employment, based not on the increased consumption that Keynes prescribed as the cure for depressions but on its restriction in favour of increased production of armaments.[7] *Mutatis mutandis*, a similar story can be told of Hitler's response to the depression: despite massive propaganda on the subject, make-work programmes and aid to agriculture actually accomplished little, and the true surge in economic activity, bringing full employment, came, as in the United States, with the preparation for and prosecution of the war.[8]

On the other hand, the limited success of the New Deal, like the later failure of the promised 'end of the business cycle' after the war, has been explained as a result of Roosevelt's reluctance fully to fill the Keynesian prescription. The New Deal programme was, after all, limited by the Supreme Court's finding the NRA national price-fixing system unconstitutional, as well as by business's opposition to increasing taxes and budget deficits, along with Roosevelt's own discomfort with the costs of state spending.[9] Resistance to the stimulus idea, in fact, has as long a history as the idea itself. Roosevelt's own Treasury Secretary, Henry Morganthau,

> believed that the failure to achieve recovery was caused by the reluctance of business to invest, because it feared federal spending would lead to inflation and heavy taxation. Since the New Deal had failed to bring the country out of the depression, the administration, he argued, should balance the budget and give business a chance to see what it could do.[10]

The history of peace-time fiscal stimulus has from the beginning been one of reluctance on the part of political-economic decision-makers, whatever the enthusiasms of theorists. Today as earlier, the standard Keynesian position is that economic contraction calls for big-time stimulus

spending, which can always be made up for by fiscal scrimp-
ing later. At the same time, as a commentator for the *New
York Times* put it, 'the idea that the world's rich countries
need to cut spending and raise taxes has a lot of truth to it'.[11]
Nothing could better convey the dilemma in which the
managers of the capitalist economy were stuck than the joint
statement issued after the conference of the G20 nations, the
world's richest, at the end of June 2010, which 'acknowledged both sides of the debate':

> There is a risk that synchronous fiscal adjustment [i. e.
> austerity measures] across several major economies
> could adversely impact the economy . . . There is also
> a risk that the failure to implement consolidation [i. e.
> impose austerity] where necessary would undermine
> confidence and growth.[12]

Dilemmas of the Mixed Economy

In the immediate post-war years the Keynesian view, enor-
mously strengthened in influence by America's success in the
war, predominated, largely because, in the words of an OECD
study, 'the expansion of the public sector took place within
an unusually stable international economic environment
and against a background of historically unprecedented rates
of economic growth'.[13] This changed in the mid-1970s, as the
rapid expansion of state economic activity in response to the
end of the Golden Age led to the emergence everywhere of
budget deficits and the new phenomenon of stagflation,
the disturbing combination of economic stagnation with
inflation. Public spending, which neither produced anew
the high growth rates of the Golden Age nor succeeded in
ending poverty, was now held to have 'detrimental effects on
resource allocation, economic incentives, consumer choice,
and individual freedom'[14] – that is, on the supposed ability

of markets to operate efficiently. More concretely, a period of reduced profitability required 'economic adjustment and flexibility'[15] – in other words, an ability to downgrade working conditions and wage levels. The 1980s saw attempts in most capitalist countries to 'reform' – that is, curtail – government spending, strikingly paralleled by moves towards the market in the 'socialist' world.

As two enthusiasts of such reform are forced to acknowledge in their survey of the question, 'relatively few countries have so far accompanied their antigovernment rhetoric with successful shifts in their policy regimes toward less state involvement and cuts in public expenditure'.[16] This was in part because much of the post-1973 increase in public spending had come in the form of 'entitlement' programmes, like old-age pensions, unemployment insurance and disability payments, which were especially difficult to cut in a time of lower growth and increasing unemployment. Education and health spending also tended not just to resist shrinkage but to increase, along with costs of industrial regulation and environmental controls. A large and growing chunk of money was required for the rising interest costs produced by growing deficits (central government expenditure on interest for the world's leading industrial nations grew from 1.4 per cent to 4.5 per cent of GDP between 1970 and 1995).[17] In fact, as one author observes, 'if debt repayment is taken together with interest payments . . . debt servicing is the largest individual item among the disproportionate increases in state expenditure in the industrial countries of the West'.[18]

In the United States, to take a spectacular example of the gap between rhetoric and reality, Ronald Reagan came to the presidency in 1980 as an animated symbol of the intention to end deficit spending and the associated inflation. Indeed, the Federal Reserve's elevation of interest rates succeeded in cutting inflation, but at the cost of a deep recession, with 10.8 per cent unemployment by the end of 1982. By 1983

118 Savings and Loans banks – heavily invested in real-estate speculation – had failed; the next year saw the bankruptcy of the nation's seventh largest bank, the Continental Illinois National Bank and Trust Company. Federal agencies bailed out the Continental Illinois to the tune of $4.5 billion, while the Savings and Loans absorbed more than $160 billion. Interest rates were lowered again, to counter the recession. And although some social spending was cut, defence expenditure soared; together with tax changes shifting the tax burden away from the richest 0.5 per cent towards middle-income earners, this resulted in an increase of the budget deficit from $80 billion (2.5 per cent of GDP) in 1981 to $200 billion (6 per cent of GDP) in 1983. By the time Reagan left office the national debt had tripled from $900 billion to $2.8 trillion.

Economic policy, in short, was not under ideological control. The other side of the same coin could be seen in the misadventures of François Mitterrand, who became the first Socialist president of post-war France in 1981. A sort of anti-Reagan, Mitterrand attempted to counter the recession that had spread worldwide from the United States by such demand-strengthening measures as 'massive investment in public works and state enterprises', along with nationalizations of private companies, a 10 per cent increase in the minimum wage, a shortening of the working week to 39 hours, five weeks of yearly paid holiday and a 'solidarity tax' on wealth. 'The result was negative. Financial markets were reluctant to help and French capital took flight abroad.'[19] Unemployment continued to grow and the franc had to be devalued three times; by 1983 the government made a decisive move in the direction of neoliberalism and focused on fighting inflation.

For the industrialized countries taken as a whole, ranging between these two extremes of ideology in conflict with reality, the mixed economy was here to stay, but increasingly eluded stabilization. The European turn to neoliberalism,[20] which led eventually to the Maastricht Treaty founding the single currency zone, had its American analogue in Bill Clinton's moves to restore budget balance, deregulate banking and 'end welfare as we know it'. But in fact it was only the government-engineered easing of credit in the US in the early 1990s that stimulated first the stock market and then the real-estate market to produce what Robert Brenner has aptly termed 'asset price Keynesianism'. Seemingly, the Reagan years had opened onto a period in which state involvement in the economy could serve private enterprise rather than rival it: military spending subsidized corporate capital; the growing interest on state debt was paid to private banks while Treasury bills, presumably proof against default, strengthened portfolios; and the easy credit facilitated by Alan Greenspan's Federal Reserve made possible a flourishing financial sector as well as the consumer spending that ultimately powered the whole world's economy. But when the great mortgage bubble collapsed in 2007, national governments found themselves caught once again between the need to keep the system functioning by pouring money into financial firms 'too big to fail', supporting local governments and 'stimulating' the private economy; and the imperative to limit the growth of state debt before it reached the point of large-scale default.

The dilemma faced by policy-makers today goes beyond the conflict between the apparent need for state support of the private economy and the quasi-instinctual revulsion at 'big government' felt by businessmen and their political representatives in the 1930s (and which can be traced back to the economic liberalism of the nineteenth century). While the need for state action in the face of the crisis that burst into the open in 2007 remains as great as in earlier moments of business collapse, today's situation is rather different from that at the outset of the Great Depression.[21] The United

States had a government debt of $16 billion in 1930; today it is $12.5 trillion and climbing. In terms of percentage of GDP, the federal debt had already reached 37.9 per cent by 1970; in 2004 it was 63.9 per cent. In that year the IMF warned that the combination of the American budget deficit and its ballooning trade imbalance threatened 'the financial stability of the global economy'; a team of Fund economists 'sounded a loud alarm about the shaky fiscal foundations of the United States, questioning the wisdom of the Bush administration's tax cuts and warning that large budget deficits pose[d] "significant risks" not just for the United States but for the rest of the world'.[22] Five years later, with even relatively modest levels of stimulus spending,

> Governments worldwide . . . are finding themselves in the same position as embattled consumers: paying higher interest rates on their rapidly expanding debt. [These rates] could translate into hundreds of billions of dollars more in government spending for countries like the United States and Germany . . . This could put unprecedented pressure on other government spending, including social programs and military spending, while also sapping economic growth by forcing up rates on debt held by companies, homeowners, and consumers.[23]

And 'even before the start of the crisis', as a recent analysis emphasizes, 'public finance in Europe was no longer sustainable, in the sense that budget balances did not improve significantly as the debt grew heavier'.[24]

The one-trillion-dollar budget passed by the Japanese parliament in March 2010, intended to stimulate an economy sunk in depression since the early 1990s, left Japan with a public debt twice the size of its GDP, the worst ratio among industrialized countries, and an interest bill amounting in

2008 to 20 per cent of the budget. A year earlier, Akito Fukunaga, a 'fixed-income strategist' for Credit Suisse, opined correctly that 'Japan will keep on selling more bonds' while worrying that 'that won't work in three to five years. If you ask me what Japan can resort to after that, my answer is "not very much."'[25] According to Moody's Investors' Service, the major bond rating agency, the United States and Britain, among other industrial nations, had by early 2010 moved 'substantially closer' to losing the AAA ratings that keeps money flowing into their government bond issues and yields low. That is, they are approaching the point at which the likelihood that they will be able to pay back loans will decline, forcing the interest rates they will have to pay to rise in response to the increased risk.

> Those higher rates, in turn, add to the country's over-all debt burden and can force the government to reduce spending, increase taxes, or both. That difficulty has been well illustrated recently in Greece and Portugal, with strikes and protests as citizens march in the streets to oppose tough austerity measures that directly reduce entitlements and state benefits.[26]

It should be added that the sovereign debt problem can appear less severe than it really is in cases like that of the United States, in which much government debt, and the painful means for counteracting it, is borne by the states rather than directly by the federal government, or that of China, in which much of the national debt is carried by provincial treasuries.

This situation poses problems to which the advocates of massive Keynesian stimulus spending have no real answer, except to promise (like Paul Krugman) that the day of reckoning for government debt is really much farther off than it may appear. As Harold G. Moulton of the Brookings

Institution pointed out long ago in a prescient critique of Keynes, the latter

> did not face the long-run fiscal implications of the resort to government spending. Unlike many of his followers, he did not specifically contend that an ever-increasing public debt is of no consequence. This fundamental long-run issue was simply ignored.[27]

A good illustration of the pertinence of Moulton's criticism is provided by Hyman P. Minsky, a Keynes follower of special interest at the present time for his insistence that the post-1960s economy was becoming increasingly vulnerable to financial crises. In his major work of 1986, Minsky blandly asserted that in 1975 the government deficit was 'offset' by a rise in personal savings and above all 'by a rise in corporate cash flows. Business profits . . . were sustained and increased even as the country was in a severe recession.'[28] This notion is based on the 'fundamental principle in economics . . . that the sum of realized financial surpluses (+) and deficits (-) over all units must equal zero'.[29] This principle seems to imply in this context, however, the illusory character of the income and profits on the credit side of the balance sheet, for they must eventually be taken to repay the amount on the governmental debit side. Of course, the unspoken assumption, for which no reasons were given, was that renewed growth would make it possible to combine this repayment with continued business expansion, thus keeping government debt 'free of default risk'.[30]

It is the looming possibility of that risk, no matter how distant it remains at present, that keeps even those in favour of stimulus spending, like the current US and Japanese governments, modest in their Keynesian ambitions, simply hoping – bolstered by economists' psychic predictions – that it will all be over in a year or two. In their hesitation between the rock of ongoing depression, with its dangers of social upheaval, and the hard place of stimulus spending, with its limited effectiveness and disastrously mounting deficits, governments seek a point of balance between their function of preserving 'social cohesion' and their fundamental orientation to the needs and wishes of business.

Hence, in the US, the Treasury Department's unwillingness to interfere seriously with bankers' decision-making about the funds shovelled in their direction; hence the seeming schizophrenia of President Obama's statement to reporters on 14 March 2009 that 'we've got to see worldwide concerted action to make sure that the massive contraction in demand [in consumer spending] is dealt with' while 'signaling to Congress', as he was reported doing a day later, that he 'could support taxing some employee health benefits', thus decreasing wages and contracting demand. And hence the unwillingness of European governments to follow the Americans very far down even this half-hearted road, leaving the stimulus exercise (with its hoped-for benefits to European exporters) to the United States while concentrating on limiting their budget deficits and tightening their citizens' belts.

If simply allowing the economy to collapse into depression, as some ultra-conservative economists seemingly urge, is one unacceptable alternative, the other is to increase the economic activity of the state radically. But the American government (federal, state and local) is already responsible for about 35 per cent of GDP. When this number hit 50 per cent at the height of the Second World War, the growth of private capital came more or less to a halt. State sector growth today would mean a similar displacement of capitalist enterprise to create a state-run economy like that of the old Soviet Union, a goal favoured by no political force (despite *Newsweek*'s 7 February 2009 scare-mongering cover story, 'We Are All Socialists Now'). It's only twenty years since Russia and its satellites embraced the free market, or at least some highly restricted version of it, but those governments show no interest in returning to the centrally planned system of yore. The Chinese state too has thrown in its lot with the market, while Cuba, long the last holdout among the centrally planned economies, reacted to the economic downturn with plans 'to lay off more than a half a million people from the public sector in the expectation that they will move into private business'.[31] Even Sweden, long the Western standard-bearer for 'socialism' in the eyes of American conservatives, refused to take over Saab from General Motors with the announcement from enterprise minister Maud Olofsson that 'The Swedish state is not prepared to own car factories.'[32] Everywhere, most stimulus money is meant to be pumped into the private economy, as income transfers, tax cuts or government payments and subsidies to businesses.

From the viewpoint of economics – including most left-wing approaches – the point of an economy is the allocation of resources to meet consumption needs. The chief issue distinguishing conflicting viewpoints, then, is what sort of economy – what mix, for example, of market and state planning – does the best job of promoting the public welfare (the wealth of nations). This is why most economists, including Keynes, think of profit-making as a device for getting people with money to invest in the production that serves consumption. And this is what allows a contemporary Keynesian like Paul Krugman to ignore the imperative of profitability and insist, in making an argument for a massive stimulus program, that 'under current conditions, a surge in public spending would employ Americans who would otherwise be unemployed and money that would otherwise be sitting idle, and put both to work producing something useful'.[33] But capitalism is a system not for providing 'employment' as an abstract goal but for employing people who produce profits; its goal is not the production of useful things but the increase of capital. (As noted above, it is an illusion embodied in the allied concepts of 'national income' and 'growth' that the health of capitalism consists in anything other than the growth of profits and so of capital investment itself.) Otherwise the fact that 'the current expansionary fiscal policy has coincided with rising, and largely unfunded, age-related spending (pension and health-care costs)'[34] would not be a *problem* requiring solution by such expedients as putting off retirement ages and, eventually, cutting benefits.

While neither economists nor businessmen have an adequate theoretical understanding of capitalism, the latter at least have a practical sense of how it works. Businessmen, however much they may claim that their activities ultimately are for the general good, know that profit itself, not consumption, is the goal of business. They can see that government-provided payments for old-age pensions, healthcare and unemployment relief represent increases in workers' incomes, not business's, and that the growing government debt will at some point have to be repaid, while in the meantime absorbing money that might have gone into business investment (whether or not in fact businesses are eager to use it in this way). They feel, without fully comprehending, the fundamental conflict between the private-enterprise economy and the government spending on which it has come to rely.[35] Broadus Mitchell's remarks about the opposition in the United States to the accumulating public debt fuelling the New Deal apply equally to the 'deficit hawks' of today, when anxiety is no more warranted by the immediate threat of fiscal insolvency than it was in the 1930s:

> There is every reason to believe that the real protest was not fiscal, but broadly economic and political in character . . . The true fear was that government, intervening in the crisis, would weaken the claims of the system of private enterprise. What began as succor to private business threatened to supplant it.[36]

The underlying problem is that government-financed production does not produce profit. This is hard to grasp, not only because it contradicts a basic presupposition of the past 75 years of economic policy – that government spending can function as an equivalent of private capitalist investment – but because a company that sells goods to the state, as when Boeing provides bombers for the Air Force, does receive a profit, and usually a good one, on its investment. But the money paid to Boeing represents a deduction from the profit produced by the economy as a whole. For the government has no money of its own; it pays with tax money or with borrowed funds that will eventually have to be repaid out of taxes.[37]

Tax money appears to be paid by everyone. But despite the appearance that business is undertaxed, only business actually pays taxes. To understand this, remember that the total income produced in a year is the money available for all purposes. Some of this money must go to replace producers' goods used up in the previous year; some must go in the form of wages to buy consumer goods so that the labour force can reproduce itself; the rest appears as profit, interest, rent – and taxes. The money workers actually get is their 'after tax' income; from this perspective, tax increases on employee income are just a way of lowering wages. The money deducted from paycheques, as well as from dividends, capital gains and other forms of business income, could appear as business profits – which, let us remember, is basically the money generated by workers' activity that they do not receive as wages – if it didn't flow through paycheques (or other income) into government coffers. So when the government buys goods or services from a corporation (or simpler yet, hands agribusiness a subsidy or a bank a bailout) it is just giving a portion of its cut of profits back to business, collecting it from all and giving it to some. The money paid to Boeing has simply been redistributed by the state from other businesses to the aircraft producer.

Government spending therefore cannot solve the problem of depression, because the problem is not insufficient consumer demand but insufficient profits for business expansion (which in turn determines the extent of consumer demand). It can put off the issue by supplying financial and other businesses with the money they need to continue operations. It can also alleviate the suffering it causes, at least in the short run, by providing jobs or money to those out of work, or create infrastructure useful for future profitable production. Beyond that, the main service rendered to the industrial capitalist system by the state, as Martin Jänicke ironically insists, is to serve as a scapegoat: while 'it is the entrepreneurs and managers who make the decisions . . . the state is blamed for failures in the economy, from inflation to unemployment, and the parties involved in the game of "changing of the guards" play it in all seriousness'.[38] The underlying problem in a period of depression can be solved only by the depression itself (perhaps aided, as on the last important occasion, by a large-scale war – a real role for the state), which (as explained in chapter Three) can raise profitability by lowering capital and labour costs, increasing productivity through technological advances and concentrating capital ownership in larger, more efficient units.

This is why the recurrent application of stimulus since the Second World War could provide an (ever weakening) simulacrum of prosperity only at the cost of a rising accumulation of debt. It is also why debt cannot expand indefinitely, without either undermining the very ability of governments to function (via the growing domination of budgets by interest charges) or diminishing the already insufficient profitability of private enterprise. It is why politicians were already turning, by mid-2010, from moderate stimulus policies to austerity, cutting government employment, unemployment relief, healthcare, pensions and everything else within reach.

6

The Future of Capitalism

In November 2009, a year into the Great Recession, the lead article in the *Guardian Weekly* did not hesitate to proclaim that 'the capitalist dream is dying a painful death'. A year and a half later such excited talk had largely disappeared from the press. Instead, stories suggesting an ongoing economic recovery sat side by side with accounts of Greece's slide towards default on its national debt, with Portugal, Spain and Great Britain possibly soon to follow. On occasion this double vision appeared in a single story, as in the *New York Times* piece about the newly instituted Homeless Prevention and Rapid Re-Housing programme responding to 'a swelling group of formerly middle-class Americans' who 'are at risk of slipping permanently into poverty, even as economic conditions improve'.[1]

Undeniably, economic affairs picked up somewhat in the United States and elsewhere in the course of 2010. To what extent was this simply the expectable result of government stimulus money, following the bailout of financial institutions? This was clearly the case with the massive state- and debt-funded infrastructure projects underway in China, but it seems just as true for the United States, despite the modest level of state expenditure there. The official theory remains the Keynesian one, that once the pump is primed the economy will shift to a higher level of activity, allowing the market once again to work its allocative magic. The flimsiness of this official theory, however, is demonstrated by the constant

83

expression of worry that the cessation of government spending will allow the 'recovering' economy to 'slip back' into recession. In the same way, and as a warning parallel, it is commonly asserted that Roosevelt's turn from stimulus to budget-balancing in 1937 nipped a burgeoning recovery in the bud, whereas surely the more straightforward explanation of the recession that followed immediately is that profitability remained too low to stimulate significant investment, a condition temporarily masked by government spending.

Even aside from the problems inherent in growing state deficits, it is as hard today as it was in the past to imagine how further infusions of government debt, aside from helping out the occasional deserving millionaire, would be able to save the world economy. What will the financiers invest in, as they become solvent again? This is the big question that is neither asked nor answered. So far, the chief option seems to be, besides the 'financial products' of yesterday's bubble economy, the bonds representing governments' growing and unredeemable debt.[2] If debt expansion for purposes of speculation could bring prosperity, we'd already be living in a new golden age. Similarly, the re-regulation of finance touted by governments and pundits as a preventive against future financial crises – even if it should go beyond the narrow limits that seem the most likely outcome of the current political brouhaha – will not solve the problem of claims on investment income far exceeding the actual money flowing to meet them, any more than pouring more freshly printed dollars into bank vaults will.

As we saw in previous chapters, the prosperity made possible by the economic and physical destruction effected by the Great Depression and the Second World War was even at its highest point, the late 1950s, insufficient to obviate the need for government stimulus. When the post-war Golden Age came to a definitive end in the mid-1970s, the massive increase in government spending that avoided a return to depression conditions then was another step on the way to today's increasingly problematic deficits. Government debt was joined by soaring amounts of corporate and private debt, making possible the apparent prosperity of the last two decades. But debt must eventually be validated – repaid – out of money made by the profitable production and sale of goods and services. Instead, the failure of the non-financial parts of the economy to expand sufficiently showed itself in 2008 in the collapse of the whole Rube Goldberg device constructed, under government auspices, out of CDOs and similar 'financial products'.

Of course, the limits of the post-1970s expansion were there to be seen all along, in the mounting unredeemable debt of Latin America and Eastern Europe, and in the millions of unemployable human beings accumulating in the slums of Africa, South Asia and Latin America, as well as in the former Soviet Union and its satellites, now liberated into the embrace of the free market. According to the UN's *Human Development Report 2004*, 'an unprecedented number of countries saw development slide backwards in the 1990s. In 46 countries people are poorer today than in 1990. In 25 countries more people are hungry today than a decade ago.'[3] In 2010 the spectre of mass poverty became inescapable in the richest nations as well: a new Japanese government acknowledged an official 16 per cent poverty rate in that fallen global number two, while growing rates of poverty, hunger and homelessness in the US demonstrated – or would have, if anyone had been interested – the utter failure of the War on Poverty fought in the waning years of the Golden Age. But such phenomena seemed then as now, incomprehensible elements of paradox, given the (business-cycle inflected) growth of GDP and the growing wealth of the minority at the top. Thus Paul Krugman, noting 'a remarkable disconnect between overall economic growth and the economic fortunes of most American families' in 2005, found this impossible to explain and pronounced it 'a mystery'.[4]

But it is only a mystery if we ignore the centrality of profit-making to the capitalist economy, and the origin of profit in the productive work performed by the employees of businesses beyond the quantity needed for their own reproduction. As far from the observable facts of economic life – the 'numbers' reported by economic specialists and journalists – as these considerations are, they are all too well confirmed by recent decades of low investment growth. If in the past it was depression itself that, by cheapening the costs of capital investment, made possible a revival in profit rates and so renewed prosperity, it is not surprising that the debt-fuelled postponement of depression should lead to stagnation, outside of the kingdom of debt, of the financial sector itself (and even here avoiding collapse has required continued infusions of government money and increasing levels of risk). If this way of looking at the economy's workings is correct – and the whole earlier history of capitalism suggests it is – there can be no real solution to the difficulties so dramatically manifested since 2007 other than the deep depression whose avoidance has been the main goal of economic policy for the last forty years.

Ignoring for the moment both the costs of economic catastrophe in human suffering and the threat this suffering might pose to what the bureaucrats call 'social cohesion', it is conceivable that such a development could lead, as in the past, to a new wind for capitalism. Deflation and bankruptcy would, as earlier in history, lower the cost of production goods, while wages would be driven down and further vast quantities of debt written off to lay the groundwork for an increased rate of profit on capital investment. The process described in this short sentence might take decades of turmoil. It would certainly involve a radical reconfiguration of the global economic system, just as the revival of capitalist prosperity that followed the deep depressions of the late nineteenth and early twentieth centuries involved the displacement of Great Britain by the United States as the dominant economic power. A world war was fought over Hitler's effort to create a unified European economy able to compete with America, and Japan's attempt to establish a similar power centre in East Asia, goals only realized, under different political auspices and with America's cooperation, after the war. The ongoing stagnation of the so-called Western economy points to similar geographic shifts if capitalism is to continue.

Most commonly this future is currently identified as emerging in China and India. In the excited words of an article for *Business Week* in 2005,

> even America's rise falls short in comparison to what's happening now. Never has the world seen the simultaneous, sustained takeoffs of two nations that together account for one-third of the planet's population. For the past two decades, China has been growing at an astounding 9.5% a year and India by 6%. . . . Barring cataclysm, within three decades India should have vaulted over Germany as the world's third-biggest economy. By mid-century, China should have overtaken the US as No. 1. By then, China and India could account for half of global output.[5]

Indeed, in 2010 China overtook Germany as the world's leading exporter. On the other hand, the *Business Week* article admits that at the moment 'China and India account for a mere 6% of global gross domestic product – half that of Japan'. More than half of all Chinese manufactured exports are produced by foreign-owned multinational firms, just as in India multinationals account for two-thirds of all sales in the leading information and computer technology sector.[6]

China's growth, in short, remains closely tied to that of the developed countries of the West, even while its importance grows as a regional hub in East Asia, where it now serves 'as the final processing and assembly platform for a large quantity of imports going from other Asian countries to Western countries through China'.[7] India, where the majority of the population still consists of poverty-stricken rural workers, is even further from being an independent economic power. Indeed 'most of the trade of the Indian and Chinese economies is still in the form of re-exports of finished or semi-finished products or services manufactured by multinational firms which are based in Europe or the US'.[8] And in both countries economic dynamism is based on external trade. Contrast this with the case of the United States, where the foundation of economic growth 'in the years 1860–1920, as in the years that followed, was a vast domestic demand' and the role of foreign trade was 'very much reduced', normally coming to no more than 4 or 5 per cent of GNP, after the Civil War, when America began its climb to industrial capitalist pre-eminence.[9]

Beyond the current, relatively undeveloped state of these possible future engines of capitalist renewal lies an even more important issue: the size of the existing capital concentrated in America, Europe and Japan, which China – and whichever other of the BRIC nations might emerge as new centres of capital accumulation – would have to drag behind them. Although *Business Week* speculated breezily about a possible 'troika of China, India, and the US', the workers of the Asian countries would have to generate the gigantic quantities of profit necessary to validate investment holdings in the rest of the world, unless the latter were simply to be written off while the restructuring of capital required for a new global prosperity brought even more radical cuts in living conditions and higher long-term unemployment in the West than those now predictable as results of the Great Recession.

Limits of Capital

Thinking of the future development of the economy in this fashion, in terms of the global accumulation of capital by private enterprises, ignores an important feature of contemporary capitalism already discussed under the heading of fiscal deficits: the increasing part played by governments (and the international organizations that act for them) in economic affairs. Recent decades have seen unrelenting efforts to undo this by privatization, self-imposed in developed countries and imposed by them (through organizations like the IMF) on developing ones. In the United States, to take an extreme example, not only has the mail service been largely moved from government to private corporate hands, but even military defence functions are now carried out to a notable extent by privately hired mercenaries. Of course, the most dramatic privatizations have been those of entire societies: the transformation of the state-directed economies of the USSR and its satellites, and with greater caution, of China, into largely market-regulated systems.[10] In the West, even apart from conscious institutional efforts toward privatization, as a useful study of the question notes, there has been an increasing

> failure of most governments to discharge those very basic functions for which the state as an institution was created – the maintenance of civil law and order, the defence of the territory . . . the guarantee of sound money to the economy, and the assurance of clear, judicially interpreted rules regarding the basic exchanges of property between buyers and sellers, lenders and borrowers, landlords and tenants.[11]

At the same time, as this author also points out, the share of GDP appropriated by the state has increased, along with 'the intrusion of governments into our daily lives'.[12] Even while more powers are abandoned by the state to profit-oriented corporations,[13] government funds, for instance in various forms of subsidy for favoured areas of business, remain essential to the operation of the economic mechanism. If it is more than an ironic turn of phrase to speak of a privatization of the state itself, as it becomes increasingly both a form of enterprise for the enrichment of its practitioners and one devoted to the servicing of dominant economic interests, it remains true that those funds represent a cost to the capitalist economy of which they have become a fundamental part.

The difficulty of lowering these costs testifies to an important fact about the evolution of society since the Great Depression: the inability to discharge state debts and the difficulty of dismantling the welfare state register the decline of the private enterprise economy as a system. Despite its dynamism and the gigantic increases in the productivity of human labour that it has achieved since the early nineteenth century, and despite the disappearance of political and social barriers to its spread in the course of the twentieth, capitalism has not been able to generate the quantities of profit required to incorporate much of the world's population into its modern industrial form. Instead, more and more profit must be diverted from capitalist purposes to feed the starving, attempt to pacify the rebellious and manage the insufficiencies of accumulation even in the developed countries. The very idea that companies like AIG, the Bank of America or Citicorp are 'too big to fail', and must be supported by government funds, amounts to a declaration of the failure of the market economy. Competition was supposed to eliminate inadequately managed firms, leaving the most productive (of profits) to prosper and thereby (according to the economists) optimizing social well-being. Blocking competition's operation amounts to admitting in practice the obsolescence of capitalism itself, just as the replacement of profitability by national income as central to economic theory represents a conceptual accommodation to this situation.

The masters of capital could, of course, act on the talk about balanced budgets and return to a strictly capitalist economic policy, instituting a true privatization. But they have not dared to do this in the period since 1945, both because of the institutionalized involvement of the state in capital as presently constituted and, in many countries, for fear of uncontrollable popular responses to the mass misery that would produce. An extreme example is provided by the neo-liberal policy, guided by the anti-Keynesian theories of Milton Friedman, imposed on the Chilean economy after the military overthrow of the Socialist government in 1973: radical cuts in public spending and mass privatizations rapidly produced an economic contraction of 15 per cent and a rise of unemployment from 3 to 20 per cent. In 1982, facing hyperinflation, exploding debt and 30 per cent unemployment, and despite its police-state powers, the Pinochet government (like its sponsor to the north at the same time) was forced to ignore ideology and nationalize many newly created private companies (Codelco, the state-owned copper producer that provided 85 per cent of Chile's export revenues, had never been denationalized). Today as well, efforts in the direction of fiscal discipline have run into barriers both in the form of large-scale public protest and in that of the de facto dependence of the economy on a certain level of government spending. Despite the incoherence of the resulting policy moves, however, the working-class majority will pay for whatever mix of stimulus and respect for market freedom governments decide upon, with lower wages and benefits or greater unemployment – in fact, as we can already see, it will be with both.

According to the 2009 OECD 'Employment Outlook', the recession had already driven the unemployment rate in the OECD area to 8.5 per cent by July of that year (Spain registered the highest rate, at 18.1 per cent), 'the steepest increase in the post-war period'. According to the same document, 'people 54 or younger are losing ground financially at an unprecedented rate', with youth unemployment a particular problem: the OECD predicted that the rate for workers between 15 and 24 years old would rise in Spain to nearly 40 per cent by 2010, in Italy and France to about 24 per cent, and in the UK and US to around 18 per cent.[14] As the *New York Times* noted early that same year, potential Asian 'smugness at having escaped losses on American subprime debt has been erased by growing despair over a plunge in sales among major exporters', leading to sharp increases in unemployment in Japan, China, Taiwan, Indonesia and other East and South Asian countries.[15]

But more significant for an understanding of the future is the likelihood, forecast by the OECD study and other analyses, that the jobs, benefits and social spending being eliminated during the recession will not come back, even with the expected recovery. Speaking of the American situation in particular, Don Peck began a long, gloomy article in *The Atlantic* by noting that while 'the Great Recession appears to be over . . . [a] return to normalcy seems far off', with unemployment not expected to fall from its current official (and certainly understated) rate of 10 per cent even by 2014. And Peck was reporting the expectations of economists, with their deep-rooted belief in the essentially upward dynamism of the market economy.[16]

Journalistic shock at the advent of long-term significant unemployment reflects lack of acquaintance with earlier recognitions of the phenomenon, in the wake of the end of the Golden Age. As a specialist on the topic observed more than a decade ago, the 'perceptible rise in unemployment in the mid-1970s marked the beginning of a new phase' in which 'elevated unemployment rates are the reflection . . . of the definite decline of the epoch of full employment'.[17]

The editor of the collection of studies in which this observation appeared introduced it by remarking that 'unemployment rates have come to depend only partly on the economic cycles', with the 1980s demonstrating that under current circumstances 'economic growth can go hand in hand with high unemployment'.[18] As a result, unemployment has come to be, to use Enrico Pugliese's word, 'nonexceptional'. 'The novelty is that people today have learned to live with unemployment rates of 10 percent and in some areas – indeed, sometimes vast areas – with even higher rates', so that high unemployment does 'not necessarily produce socially critical situations', as in the 1930s.[19] This is, of course, due not only to the long-term continuance of the situation but also to the buffers against privation furnished by government programmes, along with the fact of larger family incomes, which can cushion the blow of individual job loss.

Now it seems that American workers are going to experience the steady high joblessness that Europeans have known for 30 years, with a rather lower level of government assistance than in most European cases. Will this state of affairs become 'the new normal', as it seems to have in Europe in the recent past? As the OECD Employment Outlook noted in the 2009 report:

> Most countries have scaled up resources for labour market and social policies to support the rapidly growing number of unemployed, but additional funds are often rather limited and governments are facing difficult choices on how best to respond to the different demands.

Long-term, structural unemployment has now intersected with the return of large-dimension cyclical crisis, at a time when the choices imposed on governments by their overstretched budgets lead more and more to the dismantling of social safety-nets and cuts in state employment. The result has already been 'protests in countries as varied as Latvia, Chile, Greece, Bulgaria and Iceland, and . . . strikes in Britain and France',[20] not to mention China, the current world centre of labour unrest. These protests have taken different forms, involving greater or lesser degrees of control by political-party and trade-union organizations, for instance, and different levels of violence, and have posed varying levels of threat to the existing political system. They are all indicators of the unpredictable consequences of further moves in the direction of austerity.

Such events recall the social struggles of the 1930s, when even the relatively apolitical United States saw groups of the unemployed, sometimes mobilizing large numbers of people, taking direct and on occasion violent action to prevent evictions or loot grocery stores and distribute food, as well as demonstrating nationally and locally for government relief and supporting strikers by manning picket lines (American employers found it remarkably difficult to recruit strike-breakers even at the height of the Depression).[21] Nevertheless, as an observer and analyst who was himself an unemployed worker and activist in the 1930s has observed, 'despite the enormous unemployment the movement of the unemployed did not succeed in giving rise to real mass organizations or in activating the masses of jobless people for a long period of time, or in transforming their often spontaneously erupting expressions of dissent into political actions in the style of the labor movement'.[22] Most significantly, the social struggles in the rest of the world were no more than in the United States able to counter the drive of the dominant nations' ruling classes towards a new world war.

On the other hand, as the author just cited also contends, 'the story is fundamentally different when the misery of unemployment is accompanied by the rapid growth of general misery'.[23] An interesting recent example is to be found in the social movements that broke out in Argentina in 2001, when the working class – and much of the population as a whole – rejected the austerity imposed on them by the IMF in response to an extreme sovereign debt crisis. Unemployed organizations played an important role in driving successive governments from office.[24] But their activities took their significance from the context of a general social collapse, involving such radical measures as workers' seizure and operation of enterprises deserted by their owners. Such events, while isolated elements of the unfolding of the socio-economic disaster of which the Great Recession is the latest and so far most serious instalment, evoke the history of attempts to forge new social structures of production and distribution that in the not so distant past seemed to be part of a unified phenomenon that called itself the Left.

After the Left

The development of capitalism since the nineteenth century has involved (as Marx long ago predicted it would) the continuing transformation of the labouring population in every area of the world into wage-earning employees of capitalist firms. Although the ups and downs of the business cycle brought sometimes improvement, sometimes worsening of their working and living conditions, capitalism, given its foundation on the extraction of profit from the productive activities of workers, continually reproduces a basic conflict of interest between the working and employing classes, a conflict more recently accompanied by ecological and military threats to the continued welfare and even the existence of the human race as a whole. But the social movements and organizations that once competed or cooperated to shape that conflict into a struggle to abolish capitalism and create a new form of society in which productive labour would be free from exploitation are largely gone.

The Left that began with industrial capitalism in the 1800s, grew through the nineteenth century and reached its greatest development during the first quarter of the twentieth, no longer exists. This fact has been given recognition under many different descriptions: as the 'end of ideology', and the supposed disappearance of class as a social principle, celebrated by American sociologists in the 1950s; as the advent of 'one-dimensional man' lamented by prominent voices on the left in the late 1960s; in a particularly muddled fashion, in the 1980s, as 'post-modernism'; after the fall of Communism in the intellectually weaker form of the 'end of history'. However it is described, it is obvious that the old organizations of the Left, both larger political parties and smaller, generally more radical sects, have lost all significance as agents of social transformation, and that even the ideologies and slogans of the past have decreasing purchase on people's imaginations.

It used to be believed – this was the first great idea of the Left – that capitalism inevitably produced a working-class opposition to the system as such. Some saw this opposition as arising on moral grounds, as a response to the obvious injustices of capitalism. A more convincing idea was Marx's: he saw capitalism as a social system inherently at odds with itself, as the mechanism of money-mediated market exchange geared to the institution of private ownership of productive resources and the competitive extraction of profit clashed with the increasingly social character of production and distribution, most visible when the very success in raising the productivity of labour led to economic crisis and depression. Taking as a model the revolutionary transformations of the seventeenth and eighteenth centuries that established the social and political dominance of capitalism, he thought in terms of a conflict between the existing system, in which institutionalized social power was held by the owners of capital, and a future system of consciously socialized production existing embryonically 'within the shell' of the present. This conflict would be given conceptual form in the political consciousness of ruling class and rebellious proletariat. It would be given institutional form in working-class organizations that would ultimately contest social power with the capitalist state. As the evolution of the economic system took it from crisis to crisis, these organizations would finally be led by the experience of periodic immiseration and continual exploitation to transform themselves from structures of resistance to agents of revolution.

The idea of organization was the second great idea of the Left, shared by all ideological factions. It was embodied variously in the social-democratic party, linked with great trade unions; in the anarchist 'syndicate' or the One Big Union of the American IWW; and in the elite sect, called by history to manipulate and lead the masses of workers, common to Bakuninist anarchism and Leninism. The validity of this idea seemed visible in the spread and growth of working-class parties and unions. It was not hard to believe that struggles for reform could develop into an effort to overthrow the system as a whole, just as May Day, originally the date set in the United States for demonstrations for the eight-hour day, quickly became an international revolutionary holiday. History seemed to be moving towards the abolition of bourgeois society, as a result of its very growth; this was held by many to be visible in the transformations of capitalism itself in the direction of centralization and concentration of capital, the separation of ownership and management, and the attempt by huge national and international economic units to control aspects of the market, taken by some to prefigure the democratic regulation of the economy to come.

The illusory character of this picture was indicated by the First World War, when giant socialist organizations, fresh from pledges of international class solidarity, plunged into the war effort. This miserable debacle demonstrated that traditional workers' politics had turned out to be not a harbinger of the overthrow of capitalism but an aspect of its development, fulfilling the need for the normalization of a new mode of social relations by way of organizations capable of negotiation and compromise. It foretold their disappearance as elements of a Left in the course of the twentieth century, when the developmental phase in which they had their place – roughly, that of the initial growth of the free-enterprise system – came to an end with the growing need for state intervention.[25]

And still, the war led to revolution, in Russia, Central Europe and even in Germany, the heart of the workers' movement. These uprisings, which ended the war and threatened the radical restructuring of society, were rapidly crushed. In Europe, this was a result of the war-weary majority's unwillingness to engage in the violent defence of their interests against governing authorities; in Russia, the party dictatorship that took on the task of modernizing an underdeveloped country quickly destroyed attempts at working-class self-rule. Revolution had no place in a North America just rising to the summit of world economic power (though even here the 100,000-strong Seattle General Strike of 1919 'was seen, by both participants and opponents, as part of a process through which workers were preparing themselves to run industry and society'[26]). Yet the radically constructive activities unleashed by the disaster of the war, however short-lived, showed the independence of the revolutionary impulse from the traditional political and trade-union structures.[27]

The collapse of the world economy into massive depression a decade later led not to revolution but to a new world war, which as we have seen opened the way to a new period of capitalist expansion. In this process what had remained of the Left was swept away: into the politics of the welfare state, into sectarian insignificance or into some combination of one (or both) of these and service to the needs of the Russian state. The year 1989 brought the final disappearance of the illusion of opposition to capitalism supported by the last of these. Today, surviving elements of the Left are recognizable in such phenomena as the efforts of the Greek Communist unions to maintain a place for themselves on the political scene by controlling and channelling working-class protest, or the attempt to base a meaningful parliamentary organization in Germany on remnants of the old East German Communist Party, but nowhere do they present themselves as the potential founders of a new social world. In most countries, 'Left' has come to mean simply those political forces advocating Keynsian and income-distributed policies; and today even this wretched remnant of the historical Left is reaching its limits. In the course of this evolution, the United States, whose lack of socialist and labour movements was for so long a puzzle for commentators, has come increasingly to seem not exceptional but a precursor of today's capitalism without a Left.

The transition to capitalism, the shock of which on earlier modes of life helped give rise to the social movements of the nineteenth century, has been accomplished in much of the world. This system appears now, where it is well implanted, not as trampling on ancient ways and rights but as itself a natural order. What was once claimed polemically by Enlightenment philosophers like Adam Smith – that man is by nature a marketing animal, that individuals are endowed by their creator with inalienable individual rights to privacy and property, that with the achievement of a society based on market relations history would have reached its goal and would come to an end – has by now entered into the general consciousness as self-evident truths. Though people are as aware as ever that they live in a class society marked by oppression and exploitation, this is perceived as the natural order of things, alternatives to which appear as impossible dreams.

But although today's capitalism is in many ways a much transformed version of its nineteenth-century self, this transformation, as the Great Recession is here to remind us, has not brought an abatement of the systemic problems diagnosed in that century. If anything, the crisis looming before us is likely to be more terrible than the Great Depressions of 1873–93 and 1929–39. The continuing industrialization of agriculture and attendant urbanization of population – in 2010, it is estimated, more than half the earth's people have come to live in cities – have made more and more of the population dependent upon the functioning of the market mechanism to supply them with food and other necessities of life;[28] the existence on or over the edge of survival experienced today by the urban masses of Dakka, São Paulo and Mexico City will be echoed in the capitalistically advanced nations as unemployment and government-dictated austerity afflict more and more people not just in the developed world's Rust Belts but in New York, Los Angeles, London, Athens and Prague. And let us remember that, as we have seen, the rapidly developing crisis of sovereign debt suggests that the Keynesian card, as even a temporary solution to the problems of capitalism in crisis, has already been largely played. The new circumstances in which humanity will have to deal with capitalism's afflictions include the exhaustion of one of the main methods capitalism has found to deal with its difficulties, underlining the disappearance of the Left.

The Future of Humankind

Left to its own devices, capitalism promises economic difficulties for decades to come, with increased assaults on the earnings and working conditions of those who are still lucky enough to be wage earners around the world, waves of bankruptcies and business consolidations for capitalist firms, and increasingly serious conflicts among economic entities and even nations over just who is going to pay for all this. Which automobile companies, in which countries, will survive, while others take over their assets and markets? Which financial institutions will be crushed by uncollectable debts, and which will survive to take over larger chunks of the world market for money? What struggles will develop for control of raw materials, such as oil or water for irrigation and drinking, or agricultural land? All governments attack protectionism today (or at least they did yesterday) and call for mutual support and free trade, but in practice even a relatively integrated economic union like Europe is breaking down under the strain of divergent interests, while yesteryear's globalist cheerleaders today solemnly intone the need to Buy American.

Capitalism exists today as a world system to an unprecedented degree, especially since the breakup of the Soviet empire and the integration of the formerly centrally planned economies into the world market. Largely escaping the control of national governments, massive flows of money for both investment and speculative purposes link the fate of national economies. While this has strengthened capitalism as a system, that is internationally minded given its basis in the drive to expand money holdings by any means possible, it also means that serious problems for the system's institutions are rapidly transmitted around the globe. Any solutions to the difficulties capitalism creates for itself will likewise have to be international.

War is the traditional means to find such solutions. Will the world's people be willing to march off to war again, as in the last great crises, to secure better terms for national business interests? Europeans, whatever their governments may be planning, show every sign of having finally learned their lesson in this regard,[29] while the American popular acquiescence in war seems to have been weakened by the series of defeats and stalemates suffered in Korea, Vietnam and Iraq, and soon to be experienced in Afghanistan. Nonetheless, war continues to be a daily fact of contemporary capitalism, accounting for a major part of government budgets, and in one way or another shaping the economic, social and political existence of the global population.

Gloomy though such considerations are, they leave out two paradoxically related factors which promise further dire effects for the future of capitalism: the coming decline of oil as a source of energy and the global warming caused by the consumption of fossil fuels. 'Despite massive investments in new technologies of oil discovery and recovery', a student of the fossil-fuel system points out, 'conventional oil production [in] non-OPEC countries has been steadily falling for the past decade or more while the large OPEC producers have been unable in recent years to significantly boost their own production'.[30] This is an extremely serious matter, as fossil-fuel-based technologies have been at the heart of capitalism's expansion as a social system since the industrial revolution of the turn of the nineteenth century. It was first coal and then oil that fuelled the mechanization that raised the productivity of labour in both agriculture and industry to historically unprecedented levels and so made possible the profit to be accumulated as an increasingly massive stock of capital. Today more than ever

> Global energy inputs play an absolutely key role in keeping this vast array of machinery, transport systems, computers, lights and electricity grids going. Without a constant flow of such energy capitalist accumulation would grind to a halt.

It should also not be forgotten that oil and natural gas by-products 'are used as a feedstock in a wide variety of consumer goods, including synthetic clothing and plastic household goods, and also for a range of industrial applications as well as for power generation',[31] not to mention synthetic fertilizers and pesticides central to contemporary agriculture.

The failure seriously to address the problems implied by such facts is due in part to the technical difficulty of finding new sources of energy: most of the world's hydropower resources have already been developed; nuclear power is expensive to develop, limited by supplies of uranium and produces highly toxic waste; and the 'sources of energy that are seen as the foundation of the new "green economy" – wind power, geothermal, biofuels and photovoltaic solar energy – account for a mere 0.3 per cent, 0.2%, 0.2%, 0.04% respectively of world net energy production'.[32] It is due also to the short-term, profit-oriented nature of capitalist planning. The current economic slowdown itself, by causing a decline in oil consumption, has lowered oil prices and so both driven smaller producers out of business (notably in the US, where 20,000 oil industry employees lost their jobs in the year after 2008) and discouraged the investment required to bring new sources into development. It is clear that future generations, and that future is not too distant, will be faced with increasing difficulty in maintaining the flow of energy needed by capitalism's industrial mode of production. In the long term, this guarantees a declining productivity of labour unless – and perhaps even if – the whole system of production and distribution of goods is radically restructured. In the meantime, we can expect potentially destructive struggles among existing and emerging industrial economies for control of fuel supplies, such as the ongoing and so far inconclusive conflict over the particularly rich and relatively undeveloped oilfields of Iraq.

Maintenance of the existing energy regime, and increasing use of highly polluting fuels like coal and tar-sand oil as access to high-quality oil declines, will only exacerbate the ongoing climate change now generally accepted as caused by CO_2 emissions. Anthropogenic climate change is the result not of something as general as 'human activities' but specifically of capitalist economic growth. Population increase as such, for instance, has no statistically discernible effect on atmospheric concentrations of CO_2, but there is strong 'evidence that the annual increase in [world] GDP has a statistically significant and practically important effect on the annual change in CO_2 atmospheric concentrations'; specifically, 'a trillion dollars increase in WGDP raises CO_2 concentrations by a quantity of about half a [part per million]'. Thus the growth of WGDP 'is currently an index of the extent to which economic activity damages the environment'.[33]

But even if continuing stagnation should slow green-house gas-caused climate change, the damage already done is extremely serious; a soberly informative account by a journalist not given to exaggeration was called *Field Notes from a Catastrophe*.[34] The melting of glaciers threatens not only Swiss views but the water supplies of whole populations in such areas as Pakistan and the Andean watershed; droughts have ravaged Australian and Chinese agriculture for years now while floods periodically devastate the low-lying South Asian homes of tens of millions of people. The rolling parade of disasters is, unfortunately, only getting started; it will accompany a stagnant economy and only be exacerbated by a return to true prosperity.

What both of these ongoing social stresses promise is that the decline of the economy, however cyclically inflected, will simply be the lead-in to a crisis of the social system as such, which, because it is based on the laws of physics and chemistry, will transcend strictly economic issues.[35] If the peaking of oil supplies and the catastrophes of climate change do not provoke a major transformation of social life, then it's hard to imagine what could. This idea may seem unreal today to those of us who still live for the most part in what remains of the material prosperity wrought by postwar capitalism, much as the misery and terror of the inhabitants of war-torn Congo are hard to grasp for the inhabitants of New York or Buenos Aires. But this demonstrates only imagination's weakness, not the unreality of the challenges in store for us, as local disasters like the flood of oil that poured out from BP's drilling rig into the Gulf of Mexico in 2010 will perhaps make it easier to understand.

The biggest unknown in contemplating the future of capitalism is the tolerance of the world's population for the havoc that this social system's difficulties will inflict on their lives. That people are able to react constructively in the face of the breakdown of normal patterns of social life, improvising solutions to immediate problems of physical and emotional survival, is amply demonstrated by their behavior in the face of disasters like earthquakes, floods and wartime devastation. Charles E. Fritz, who as a captain in the US Army was stationed in Britain during the Second World War, studied the reactions of German civilians to the terror bombing of German cities by the Allies and in 1950 became associate director of the University of Chicago's Disaster Research Project. In his writings Fritz emphasized the socially and psychologically positive reaction of people to disasters, observing that:

> The widespread sharing of danger, loss, and deprivation produces an intimate, primarily group solidarity among the survivors, which overcomes social isolation, provides a channel for intimate communication and expression, and provides a major source of physical and emotional support and reassurance . . . Disaster provides a form of societal shock which disrupts habitual, institutionalized patterns of behavior and renders people amenable to social and personal change . . . People see the opportunity for realizing certain wishes that remained latent and unfulfilled under the old sysytem . . . [such as] the possibility of wiping out old inequalities and injustices.[36]

Observing that the 'traditional contrast between "normal" and "disaster" almost always ignores or minimizes [the] recurrent stresses of everyday life', Fritz recognized 'a historically consistent and continually growing body of political and social analyses that points to the failure of modern societies to fulfill an individual's basic human needs for community identity'.[37] As Rebecca Solnit, who rediscovered Fritz's work in the course of her own studies of people's reactions to disaster, observes:

> An economic disaster is on the face of it not at all like a natural disaster. What has been wrecked is immaterial and abstract, but its consequences are more than tangible: it creates hardships, even emergencies, upends everyday life, throws people together in unexpected ways, changes their status, and often prompts them to take collective action.[38]

It is clear that people are going to have adequate opportunity to explore such possibilities in the near future, if they wish to better their conditions of life in the concrete ways an unravelling economy will require. While at present they are still awaiting the promised return of prosperity, at some point the newly homeless millions, like many of their predecessors in the 1930s, may well look at foreclosed, empty houses, unsaleable consumer goods and stockpiled government foodstuffs and see the materials they need to sustain life. The simple taking and use of housing, food and other goods, however, by breaking the rules of an economic system based on the exchange of goods for money, in itself implies a radically new mode of social existence.

The social relation between employers and wage-labourers, one that joins mutual dependence to inherent conflict, has become basic to all the world's nations. It will decisively shape the ways the future is experienced and responded to.

No doubt, as in the past, workers will demand that industry or governments provide them with jobs, but if the former could profitably employ more people, they would already be doing so, while the latter are even now coming up against the limits of sovereign debt. As unemployment continues to expand, perhaps it will occur to workers with and without jobs that factories, offices, farms, schools and other workplaces will still exist, even if they cannot be run profitably, and can be set into motion to produce goods and services that people need. Even if there are not enough *jobs* – paid employment, working for business or the state – there is plenty of *work* to be done if people organize production and distribution for themselves, outside the constraints of the business economy.

Such vast alterations in social relations would naturally encounter resistance from those who economically and politically dominate the existing system. They have concrete powers and privileges to lose, even if in a general way the end of capitalism would ultimately improve life for all. ('In the long run', as Keynes famously observed, 'we are all dead'.) Rebecca Solnit, in her study of reactions to disaster, notes the recurrent opposition of state authorities to citizens' efforts to organize mutual aid in the face of disaster. Even when the goal is simply survival, and not the radical transformation of society, governments send in police and military forces to prevent the elaboration of grass-roots self-help organizations. As in totalitarian states, so also in democratic ones the formation of popular authorities poses an immediate threat to the powers that be, however limited the ambitions of the people concerned. Threats to the economic order will certainly be met with repression, going beyond the military and police violence already mobilized in recent years against anti-austerity demonstrators in Athens, striking government workers in South Africa, students in London and elsewhere and the growing number of activists produced by brutal employment conditions in China.

On the other hand, the 'other world' whose possibility poses such a threat to the rulers of the present one is not just a nice idea, but has a real basis in the existing social system. In the world capitalism has created, as Adam Smith pointed out in 1776, when it was just getting under way, the well-being of each individual is systematically dependent on the activity of others. This web of interdependency now operates through the market exchange of goods for money, but it exists equally in the very mechanics of a system in which production technologies require steady flows of raw materials, energy and workers from other units in the system to produce vast quantities of goods and services for what is ultimately a global mass of consumers. What nineteenth-century social visionaries called the 'commonwealth of labour' actually exists; but this existence is obscured by the network of market exchanges that both duplicates and obscures the physical system of production and distribution.

When the financial shit hit the fan in late 2007, everyone with access to the media, in the United States at least, from the President to left-wing commentators like Doug Henwood of the *Left Business Observer*, agreed that it was necessary to save the banks with infusions of government cash lest the whole economy collapse. But, aside from the fact that the economy declined into depression anyway, the opposite is closer to the truth: if the whole financial system fell away, and money ceased to be the power source turning the wheels of production, the whole productive apparatus of society – machines, raw materials and above all working people – would still be there, along with the human needs it can be made to serve. The sooner people come to understand this, the better, because confronting the disasters inherent in long-term economic stagnation, or worse, especially in combination with ecological catastrophes, will eventually require no less than the construction of a new system for producing and distributing goods and services.

In relation to such possible developments, there is a positive aspect to the disappearance of the Left historically; Left organizations, seeing their own existence and influence as central to the success of any revolutionary struggle, typically obstructed the exploration of new ideas and modes of action by activated masses of people. But, in any case, the main forms of organized Left activity – the parties, unions and radical sects that had roles, sometimes important ones, to play in the development of modern capitalism – have lost those roles. People will therefore have to develop new forms of organized activity, if they are to respond to the ongoing collapse of capitalism by constructing a new social system. Nineteenth-century names like 'socialism', 'communism' and 'anarchism', tied to the now-defunct Left whose inspiring visions have been historically entwined with conceptual inadequacies and institutional monstrosities, may no longer be useful for naming this new system, the other world anti-globalist protesters call for, which is as necessary for human welfare as it is possible. Whatever it is called, it will need to begin by abolishing the distinction between those who control and those who perform the work of production, by replacing a social mechanism based on monetary market exchange (including the buying and selling of the ability to work) with some mode of shared social decision-making adequate to a global economic system. Even if the economic difficulties inherent in capitalism would thus be obviated, the ecological problems capitalism has created would of course remain, requiring full application of the creative human energies a radical social transformation would unleash. But it is clear that the precondition for a desirable human future requires us to move beyond the increasingly dysfunctional system, subordinated to the imperative of private profit-making and capital accumulation, through whose most recent crisis we are now living.

References

Preface

1 James K. Galbraith, 'Who Are These Economists, Anyway?', *Thought & Action*, 25 (2009), p. 95.

2 Galbraith dismisses contemporary Marxists for their 'focus on the "real economy", as opposed to finance, which 'means that the radical tradition does not truly provide a theory of *financial* crisis' (ibid., pp. 88–9). However true this may be for today's Marxists – the distinction between 'real' and 'financial economy' really derives from Keynes, a major influence on academic Marxist economics – it does not hold for Marx himself.

3 For anyone in danger of taking economic statistics for literal truths, Oskar Morgenstern's classic *On the Accuracy of Economic Observations*, 2nd edn (Princeton, NJ, 1963) is indispensable.

1 What Happened?

1 Richard A. Posner, the US appeals court judge and economic pundit, called the downturn a depression in his book, *A Failure of Capitalism*; more significantly, economists Barry Eichengreen and Kevin H. O'Rourke insisted in 2009, on the basis of a careful review of data, that 'it's a depression alright', pointing out that '[f]ocusing on the US causes one to minimize [the] alarming fact' that 'globally we are tracking or doing worse than the Great Depression' (At www.voxeu.org/index.php?q=node/3421, last accessed 10 November 2010).

2 Paul Krugman, 'Reform or Bust', *New York Times* (20 September 2009). It was with more solicitude for banks that Fed chairman Bernanke described the Obama government's decision to limit salaries at some financial firms receiving federal handouts as a way 'to ensure that compensation packages appropriately tie rewards

to longer-term performance and do not create undue risks for the firm or the financial system'. 'Fed to Monitor Pay of Bankers to Curtail Risk', *New York Times* (23 October 2009), p. 1.

3 The idea of an undervalued renminbi, much harped upon in American economic commentary, may in fact be something of an exaggeration; see Tao Wang, 'Exchange Rate Dynamics', in Eswar Prasad, ed., *China's Growth and Integration into the World Economy: Prospects and Challenges* (Washington, DC, 2004), pp. 21–8.

4 'Asia's Revenge', *Financial Times* (8 October 2008).

5 Martin Wolf, *Why Globalization Works* (New Haven, CT, 2004), p. 184.

6 Robert E. Lucas Jr, 'Mortgages and Monetary Policy', *Wall Street Journal* (19 September 2007), p. 20.

7 For example, 'Post-Keynesian' economist Paul Davidson argued that while 'Keynes won the policy battles of the first three decades after the publication of *The General Theory*', in terms of dominant theory "Keynesians" had erected a 'neo-classical synthesis' micro-foundation to Keynes's macroeconomics which could not logically support Keynes's general case'; *International Money and the Real World*, 2nd edn (New York, 1992), p. 66. While true, this did not prevent Paul Samuelson, leading producer of the neoclassical synthesis, from garnering a Nobel Prize, top status among professional economists, and a large extra income from his widely assigned economics textbook.

8 At www.nytimes.com/2009/09/06/magazine/06Economic-t.html (last accessed 20 December 2010)

9 *Financial Times* (5 August 2009).

10 Todd A. Knoop, *Recessions and Depressions: Understanding Business Cycles* (Westport, CT, 2004), p. 125.

11 G. Cooper, *The Origin of Financial Crises* (New York, 2008), p. 93.

12 For brief versions of the argument, see David Kotz, 'Crisis and Neoliberal Capitalism', Robert Pollin, 'We're All Minskyites Now' and Steve Keen, 'The "Credit Tsunami"', in Gerald Friedman et al., *The Economic Crisis Reader: Readings in Economics, Politics, and Social Policy from Dollars & Sense* (Boston, MA, 2009), pp. 34–50.

13 David Harvey, *The Enigma of Capital and the Crises of Capitalism* (London, 2010), p. 117. More or less the same argument is made by Engelbert Stockhammer in 'Neoliberalism, Income Distribution and the Causes of the Crisis', *Research on Money and Finance*,

19 (at www.researchonmoneyandfinance.org/discussion-papers, last accessed 10 November 2010) and, without Marxist flourishes, by former Secretary of Labor Robert Reich in 'How to End the Great Recession', *New York Times* (3 September 2010), p. A21. For a discussion of Harvey's confusion of Marxian and Keynesian theory, see my review of his *The Limits to Capital*, in *Historical Materialism*, 16 (2008), pp. 205–32.

14 'China raises estimate of economic growth in 2009 to 9.1%', *New York Times* (3 July 2010), p. B2; Brice Pedroletti, 'Quand la Chine se ruinera . . .', *Le Monde* (22 June 2010), p. 3.

15 Robert Brenner, *Economía de la turbolencia global* (Madrid, 2009); an English version of the prologue to this publication, from which I quote, is available at http://escholarship.org/uc/item/0sg0782h under the title 'What is Good for Goldman Sachs is Good for America: The Origins of the Current Crisis' (last accessed 10 November 2010), p. 62.

2 Ups and Downs

1 Cited by the Baltimore *Niles Weekly Register*, XLVIII/1233 (9 May 1835), pp. 167–8; in John Sperling, *Great Depressions, 1837–1844, 1893–1898, 1929–1939* (Glenview, IL, 1966), p. 26.

2 Ibid., p. 32.

3 Ibid., p. 57.

4 For a good introduction, see Maurice Flamant and Jeanne Singer-Kérel, *Modern Economic Crises and Recessions* (New York, 1970).

5 Commentators give different dates for the duration of the Great Depression. With reference to the US, for example, some interpret the upturn of 1933 as its conclusion, to be followed by another recession in 1937–8; others, ascribing the 1933–6 recovery to three years of government stimulus spending, find the true end of the depression in the expansion made possible by the start of massive war production in 1939. Of course, the latter was, economically speaking, just another form of stimulus, though one more acceptable than earlier New Deal measures because it funnelled money to corporations rather than directly to jobless workers, and because the war laid the basis for American dominance of the world economy. It was not until 1946 that the capitalist economy was once more able to expand without essential

dependence on government spending. For an outstanding history, see Broadus Mitchell, *Depression Decade: From New Era through New Deal, 1929–1941* (New York, 1947).

6 Todd A. Knoop, *Recessions and Depressions. Understanding Business Cycles* (Westport, CT, 2004), pp. 8, 3.

7 Prix Bordin, Section d'économie politique et statistique, *Académie des sciences morales et politiques, Séances et travaux* (Paris, 1860), p. 186.

8 C. Juglar, *Des Crises Commerciales et de leur retour périodique in France, en Angleterre, et aux États-Unis* (Paris, 1862), p. vii.

9 Gottfried von Haberler, *Prosperity and Depression: A Theoretical Study of Cyclical Movements* (Geneva, 1937).

10 J.-C.-L. Simonde de Sismondi, *New Principles of Political Economy: Of Wealth in Its Relation to Population*, trans. Richard Hyse (New Brunswick, NJ, 1991), p. 2.

11 George A. Akerlof and Robert J. Schiller, *Animal Spirits: How Human Psychology Drives the Economy, and Why It Matters for Global Capitalism* (Princeton, NJ, 2009).

12 Christina Romer, 'Business Cycles', *The Concise Encyclopedia of Economics*, at www.econlib.org/library/Enc/BusinessCycles.html (last accessed 20 December 2010).

13 Haberler, *Prosperity and Depression*, pp. 167–68.

14 Michael von Tugan-Baranowski, *Studien zur Theorie und Geschichte der Handelskrisen in England* (Jena, 1901).

15 W. C. Mitchell, *Business Cycles: The Problem and Its Setting* (New York, 1927), pp. 2, 1.

16 Ibid., p. 2.

17 Ibid., p. 75.

18 Ibid., p. 106.

19 Ibid., p. 107.

20 One reason for the iffy nature of economic statistics is the highly theory-driven nature of many of the calculations involved in the creation of GDP data; for example, owner-occupied housing is treated as 'worth' the amount that would have been paid to rent it. In this connection, chapter Fourteen, 'National Income Statistics', in Oskar Morgenstern, *On the Accuracy of Economic Observations*, 2nd edn (Princeton, NJ, 1963), is particularly instructive.

21 Economics began, in fact, with the study of the economy as a whole, most notably in the works of the French 'Physiocrats', who

influenced the classical economists in their attempts to understand the conditions regulating the 'wealth of nations', as Adam Smith called what is now known as national income. Classical theory was in turn the stepping-off point for Marx's analysis of capitalist economic development. Keynes's macroeconomics was thus a novelty only in relation to the neoclassical restriction of inquiry to the economic behaviour of individual households and firms.

22 John M. Keynes, *The General Theory of Employment, Interest, and Money* (New York, 1936), pp. 23–4.

23 Ibid., p. 27.

24 Philip Mirowski, *More Heat Than Light. Economics as Social Physics, Physics as Nature's Economics* (Cambridge, 1989), p. 307. Or, in the words of an earlier account, 'By stressing consumption and income, [Keynes] in effect removed the spotlight from the determinants of investment and accumulation, the phenomena which every major theorist before him had identified as the critical variables in macroeconomic instability'; Philip Mirowski, *The Birth of the Business Cycle* (New York, 1985), p. 113.

25 Mitchell, *Business Cycles*, pp. 145, 173.

26 Ibid., p. 173. In an earlier book, Mitchell explained crises as produced when 'profit margins are threatened by the encroachments of costs, when these encroachments cannot be offset by further advances in selling prices, and when the rate at which profits are capitalized is reduced by the rise in interest', without explaining why these negative factors are bound to operate recurrently; Wesley C. Mitchell, *Business Cycles and Their Causes* [1913] (Berkeley and Los Angeles, CA, 1941), p. 71.

27 Hyman P. Minsky, 'The Financial Instability Hypothesis' [1977], in *Can 'It' Happen Again? Essays on Instability and Finance* (Armonk, NY, 1982), pp. 63, 65. Minsky appears unaware that what he considers his theory of financial instability was elaborated already in 1913 by Mitchell, who similarly located the trigger for crisis in the inability of businesses to secure new loans in the face of falling profits.

28 Oliver Blanchard, Changyong Rhee and Lawrence Summers, 'The Stock Market, Profit, and Investment', *Quarterly Journal of Economics* (February 1993), pp. 115-136.

29 José A. Tapia Granados, 'Economists, Recessions, and Profits', *Capitalism, Nature, Socialism*, XXI/1 (2010), pp. 115–116.

3 Money, Profit and Cycles

1 We might just as well have consulted *The Penguin Dictionary of Economics* by G. Bannock, R. E. Baxter and R. Rees (2nd edn, Harmondsworth, 1978): Money is 'anything which is generally acceptable as a means of settling debt', while debt is a 'sum of money or other property owed by one person or organization to another'.

2 Adam Smith, *The Wealth of Nations*, vol. 1 (Oxford, 1976), pp. 22–3.

3 Ibid., pp. 26–7.

4 Thorstein Veblen, *The Theory of Business Enterprise* [1904] (New York, 1965), pp. 84–5.

5 Readers acquainted with the critique of political economy will recognize in the above an (extremely condensed) restatement of Karl Marx's analysis of money in capitalism; see *Contribution to the Critique of Political Economy* (various editions) and *Capital*, 1/1 (various editions). For an extremely lucid explanation of Marx's ideas, see Martha Campbell, 'Marx's Theory of Money: A Defense', in *New Investigations of Marx's Method*, ed. Fred Moseley and Martha Campbell (Atlantic Highlands, NJ, 1997), pp. 89–120, and 'The Credit System', in *The Culmination of Capital: Essays on Volume III of Marx's 'Capital'*, ed. Martha Campbell and Geert Reuten (London, 2002), pp. 212–27.

6 Veblen, *The Theory of Business Enterprise*, p. 85.

7 Marx notes that because of the dynamic complexity of the economic system this feature of money is 'not a defect'; 'on the contrary, it makes this [representation] the adequate one for a mode of production whose laws can only assert themselves as blindly operating averages between constant irregularities'; *Capital*, vol. 1, trans. Ben Fowkes (Harmondsworth, 1976), p. 196.

8 It is for this reason that Marx invented the concept of 'surplus value' to signify the excess over the production costs, in social labour time, of goods and services, treating profit, interest and rent as portions of this quantity.

9 Interest rates, measuring a deduction from business profits to pay for borrowed money, can in contrast be manipulated to a degree by government authorities, apart from their responsiveness to the forces of supply and demand for loans.

10 Angus Maddison, *Monitoring the World Economy, 1820–1992*

(Paris, 1995), p. 36. To take a particularly striking example of this development, the General Motors factory in Lordstown, Ohio cost \$100 million to build in 1966, when it was the most automated automobile factory in the world; in 2002, GM spent \$500 million to modernize the plant, which permitted reducing the workforce from 7,000 to 2,500.

11 See Marx, *Capital*, III/3 (various editions).

4 After the Golden Age

1 Maurice Flamant and Jeanne Singer-Kérel, *Modern Economic Crises and Recessions* (New York, 1970), pp. 76–7.

2 Barry Eichengreen, *The European Economy Since 1945: Coordinated Capitalism and Beyond* (Princeton, NJ, 2007), pp. 55, 56.

3 Ibid., p. 58.

4 Ibid., pp. 55, 59.

5 In South Korea, similarly, 'foreign assistance – mostly US aid – provided more than half the total resources available for capital accumulation in every year from 1955 to 1962 . . .': Steven R. Shalom, 'Capitalism Triumphant?' in *Zeta*, 1989, p. 95.

6 Angus Maddison, *The World Economy in the 20th Century* (Paris, 1989), p. 34.

7 Tom Kemp, *The Climax of Capitalism: The US Economy in the Twentieth Century* (London, 1990), p. 132.

8 In economist-bureaucratese: 'Increased expenditure on income maintenance reflects those concerns for social solidarity and consensus-building which have found expression in the maturing of the welfare state': Peter Saunders and Friedrich Klau, *The Role of the Public Sector*, OECD Economic Studies, 4 (1985), p. 19.

9 Maddison, *The World Economy*, p. 69.

10 Philip A. Klein, *Business Cycles in the Postwar World: Some Reflections on Recent Research*, Domestic Affairs Study, 42 (Washington, DC, 1976), pp. 2–3.

11 For a detailed account, see Herbert Stein, *The Fiscal Revolution in America* (Chicago, IL, 1969), chaps 11–13.

12 Joyce Kolko, *Restructuring the World Economy* (New York, 1988), p. 19.

13 William D. Nordhaus, 'The Falling Share of Profits', *Brookings Papers on Economic Activity*, 1 (Washington, DC, 1974), p. 169.

Cp. T. P. Hill, *Profits and Rates of Return* (Paris, 1979). In 'Is the Rate of Profit Falling?' Martin Feldstein and Lawrence Summers used rather unconvincing methods to argue against the conclusion from their own data of a small but steady trend decline in profitability between 1948 and 1976; while noting that '1970 to 1976 has generally been a period of unusually low rates of return' they speculated hopefully that 'the fall in the return is itself likely to be temporary' (paper presented at the Brookings Panel on Economic Activity in April 1977, pp. 23, 26).

14 Eichengreen, *The European Economy*, p. 271.

15 Hyman P. Minsky, *Stabilizing an Unstable Economy* [1986], (New York, 2008) pp. 17–18, 27, 31.

16 Kemp, *The Climax of Capitalism*, p. 184.

17 *New York Times* (13 July 1986).

18 See Joseph A. Pechman, *Who Paid the Taxes, 1966–85* (Washington, DC, 1985).

19 Robert Brenner, 'What is Good for Goldman Sachs is Good for America: The Origins of the Current Crisis', p. 6.

20 See Kolko, *Restructuring the World Economy*, p. 70.

21 Paolo Giussani, 'Empirical Evidence for Trends Toward Globalization. The Discovery of Hot Air', *International Journal of Political Economy*, XXVI/3 (1996), p. 31.

22 Though, as enthusiast of globalization Martin Wolf notes, 'globalization is considerably more limited than [its] critics suppose. In some respects the global economic integration is no more than it was a century ago before the breakdown that occurred between 1914 and 1945. In some ways it is considerably less': *Why Globalization Works* (New Haven, CT, 2004), p. 95. For data confirming this judgement, see Giussani, 'Empirical Evidence'.

23 Giussani, 'Empirical Evidence', p. 30. In 2006 two-thirds of total global foreign direct investment went to developed economies; the European Union alone accounted for 40 per cent of global FDI: Philip McCann, 'Globalization, Multinationals, and BRICS', in *Globalization and Emerging Economies: Brazil, Russia, India, Indonesia, China and South Africa*, ed. Raed Safadi and Ralph Lattimore (Paris, 2008), p. 91.

24 McCann, 'Globalization, Multinationals, and BRICS', p. 84.

25 Celso Furtado, 'Transnationalization and Monetarism', *International Journal of Political Economy*, XVII/1 (1987), p. 30.

26 Quoted in Jonathan R. Laing, 'The Bubble's New Home', *Barron's* (20 June 2005).

5 Appropriate Policies

1 'When Will the Recession Be Over?' *New York Times* (1 March 2009), p. 12.

2 See, for example, 'No Clear Accord on Stimulus By Top 20 Industrial Nations', *New York Times* (15 March 2009), p. 1.

3 'Pledges to Aid Weak Nations in Europe Near $1 Trillion': *New York Times* (10 May 2010), p. 3.

4 'A Trillion for Europe, With Doubts Attached', *New York Times* (11 May 2010), p. B4.

5 'While Everyone Fiddles', *New York Times* (13 March 2009), p. 26.

6 As did the more than 200 economists, including Nobel laureates James Buchanan, Edward Prescott and Vernon Smith, who signed an advertisement appearing in the *New York Times* on 28 January 2009: 'Notwithstanding reports that all economists are now Keynesians and that we all support a big increase in the burden of government, we do not believe that more government spending is a way to improve economic performance. More government spending by Hoover and Roosevelt did not pull the United States economy out of the Great Depression in the 1930s . . . Lower tax rates and a reduction in the burden of government are the best ways of using fiscal policy to boost growth.'

7 Hence Paul Krugman's cheery economist's description of the effect of the war, with its 50–60 million dead, as 'the miracle of the 1940s'. *New York Times* (6 September 2010), p. A19. See Paul Mattick, 'The Great Depression and the New Deal', in *Economics, Politics, and the Age of Inflation* (London, 1978), pp. 114–42.

8 See Adam Tooze, *The Wages of Destruction: The Making and Breaking of the Nazi Economy* (New York, 2006), esp. pp. 62–5, 206.

9 'While Roosevelt had broken with the budget-balancers and resumed spending, he still [in 1938] had not embarked on the kind of massive spending which the Keynesians called for . . . The Keynesian formula for gaining prosperity by deliberately creating huge deficits year after year seemed to defy common sense.

Roosevelt was willing to contemplate limited, emergency spending, but halfway measures of this sort antagonized business and added to the public debt without giving a real fillip to the economy': William E. Leuchtenburg, *Franklin D. Roosevelt and the New Deal* (New York, 1963), p. 264.

10 Ibid., p. 244.

11 David Leonhardt, 'Pulling Back, amid Echoes of the 1930s' *New York Times* (30 June 2010), p. 3.

12 'G-20 Countries Agree to Halve Their Budget Deficits', *New York Times* (28 June 2010), p. B7.

13 Peter Saunders and Friedrich Klau, *The Role of the Public Sector: Causes and Consequences of the Growth of Government*, OECD Economic Studies 4 (1985), p. 11.

14 Ibid., p. 12.

15 Ibid., p. 13.

16 Vito Tanzi and Ludger Schuknecht, *Public Spending in the 20th Century: A Global Perspective* (Cambridge, 2000), p. 20.

17 Ibid., p. 46.

18 Martin Jänicke, *State Failure: The Impotence of Politics in Industrial Society*, trans. Alan Braley (University Park, PA, 1990), p. 78.

19 Susan Strange, *The Retreat of the State: The Diffusion of Power in the World Economy* (Cambridge, 1996), p. 76.

20 *Pace* Martin Wolf, for whom the word 'is an incomprehensible piece of neo-Marxist jargon' (*Why Globalism Works*, p. 95), 'neo-liberalism' works as well as any other term to refer to the post-war combination of *laissez-faire* ideology (and a rather high level of openness on trade and finance) with historically high levels of state involvement in the economy and an important economic role played by international entities like the World Bank and the IMF.

21 As a study prepared for the Bank for International Settlements put it, 'the existence of a higher level of public debt is likely to reduce both the size and the effectiveness of any future fiscal response to an adverse shock. Since policy cannot play its stabilizing role, a more indebted economy will be more volatile. This was evident during the latest crisis': Stephen G. Cecchetti, M. S. Mohanty and Fabrizio Zampoli, 'The Future of Public Debt: Prospects and Implications', BIS Working Papers, 300 (March 2010), p. 14.

22 'IMF Warns That US Debt Is Threatening Global Stability', *New York Times* (8 January 2004), p. 1.

23 'Rising Interest on Nations' Debt May Sap Growth', *New York Times* (4 June 2009).

24 Thomas Brand and Marcos Poplawski Ribeiro, 'La soutenabilité des finances publiques', in *L'économie mondiale 2010*, ed. CEPII (Paris, 2009), p. 72.

25 'Sinking in Debt', *New York Times* (21 October 2009), p. B4.

26 'Moody's Says US Debt Could Test Triple-A Rating', *New York Times* (16 March 2010), p. B1.

27 Harold G. Moulton, *Controlling Factors in Economic Development* (Washington, DC, 1949), p. 136.

28 Hyman P. Minsky, *Stabilizing an Unstable Economy*, p. 31.

29 Ibid., p. 30.

30 Ibid., p. 39.

31 In the words of President Raúl Castro, 'We have to erase forever the notion that Cuba is the only country in the world where one can live without working.' 'Cuba's Public-Sector Layoffs signal Major Shift', *New York Times* (14 September 2010), p. A1.

32 'Saab on the Brink as Swedish Crisis Reaches Deadlock', *The Telegraph* (19 February 2009).

33 Paul Krugman, 'Fighting Off Depression', *New York Times* (4 January 2009).

34 Cecchetti et al., 'The Future of Public Debt', p. 6.

35 Hence the conclusion of the BIS economists that 'persistently high levels of public debt will drive down capital accumulation, productivity growth and long-term potential growth' (ibid., p. 16). According to IMF analysts in the so-called recovery year of 1985, the years after 1983 saw 'historically unusual proportions of private saving being absorbed by the financing of government deficits . . . [and] significantly lower proportions absorbed by gross private domestic investment . . . than during earlier recoveries': International Monetary Fund, *World Economic Outlook 1985*, pp. 102–3.

36 Broadus Mitchell, *Depression Decade: From New Era through New Deal, 1929–1941* (New York, 1947), p. 48.

37 For a thorough exploration of this issue, see Paul Mattick, *Marx and Keynes: The Limits of the Mixed Economy* (Boston, MA, 1967).

38 Jänicke, *State Failure*, pp. 24–5. 'Of course', Jänicke adds, 'they get the credit if the economy prospers' (p. 25).

6 The Future of Capitalism

1 'US Offers a Hand to Those On Eviction's Edge', *New York Times* (22 April 2010), p. 1.

2 In a surrealistically poetic development, some investors have found a speculative opening in the very threat of capitalistically generated catastrophe: 'Investors, still reeling from one disaster, are betting on the likelihood of another. Amid the volatility in the markets, wealthy individuals and big institutions are flocking to hedge funds that buy so-called catastrophe bonds and other investments tied to the probability of Gulf Coast hurricanes, Japanese earthquakes, large snowfalls in Canada and other natural disasters.' 'Looking to Diversify, Investors Bet on Catastrophe Bonds', *New York Times* (7 January 2011), p. B4.

3 Cit. Mike Davis, *Planet of Slums* (London, 2006), p. 163.

4 Paul Krugman, 'The Joyless Economy', *New York Times* (5 December 2005).

5 'A New World Economy: The balance of power will shift to the East as China and India evolve', *Business Week* (22 August 2005). The numbers are more indicative than exact; the IMF pegs China's growth at 'almost 8 percent': Eswar Prasad and Thomas Rumbaugh, 'Overview', in *China's Growth and Integration into the World Economy. Prospects and Challenges*, ed. Eswar Prasad (Washington, DC, 2004), p. 1, while an OECD researcher figured China's growth rate at 10.2 per cent and India's at 9.2 per cent in 2005: Philip McCann, 'Globalization, Multinationals, and BRICS', in *Globalization and Emerging Economies: Brazil, Russia, India, Indonesia, China and South Africa*, ed. Raed Safadi and Richard Lattimore (Paris, 2008), p. 99.

6 McCann, 'Globalization', p. 77.

7 Prasad and Rumbaugh, 'Overview', p. 1.

8 McCann, 'Globalization', pp. 77, 103.

9 Peter d'A. Jones, *The Consumer Society: A History of American Capitalism* (Harmondsworth, 1965), p. 173.

10 P. S. Filipov, an economist elected to the Leningrad city council in 1990, expressed the new spirit with elegant concision when he agreed 'with those who say we must hurry quickly away from Marxism-Leninism, through Socialism, to Reaganism': *New York Times* (24 June 1990), p. 1.

11 Susan Strange, *The Retreat of the State: The Diffusion of Power in the World Economy* (Cambridge, 1996), p. xii.

12 Ibid., p. xi.

13 Thus Strong argues that multinational enterprises have become de facto political entities, with effects on state policies outweighing the power of governments to regulate them (for example, with respect to taxation), a 'shift from state authority to market authority' that 'has been in large part the result of state policies'; ibid., p. 44).

14 At www.oecd.org/els/employment/outlook, last accessed on 12 November 2010.

15 'Unemployment Surges around the World, Threatening Stability', *New York Times* (15 February 2009), p. 1.

16 For example, Mark Zandi, chief economist of Moody's Economy.com, who predicted a 'permanently higher' unemployment rate, found no better explanation than that 'the collective psyche has changed as a result of what we've been through'. Don Peck, 'How a New Jobless Era Will Transform America', *The Atlantic* (March 2010).

17 Enrico Pugliese, 'The Europe of the Unemployed', *International Journal of Political Economy*, XXIII/3 (1993), p. 15. The year 1986 saw the publication of John Keane's and John Owens's book *After Full Employment*. Japan's relatively low unemployment figures during this period – though the 2.9 per cent measured at the end of 1985 was the highest since records began to be kept in 1953 – reflect the peculiarities of the Japanese definition of employment, which counts as employed laid-off workers, people who worked more than one hour of the last week of each month and soldiers, and counts as unemployed only those who have lost full-time work (see Joyce Kolko, *Restructuring the World Economy* (New York, 1988), p. 336). Kazumichi Goka, 'Unemployment and Irregular Unemployment Under Restructuring in Today's Japan', *International Journal of Political Economy*, XXIX/1 (1999), pp. 49–64, provides a survey of the effects on employment of the Japanese depression of the 1990s; among the rare treatments of the limits of the post-war Japanese 'economic miracle' as workers experienced them is Satoshi Kamata, *Japon: l'envers du miracle*, trans. Danielle Nguyen Duc Long (Paris, 1982).

18 Martin Kronauer, 'Unemployment in Western Europe', *International Journal of Political Economy*, XXIII/3 (1993), p. 3.

19 Pugliese, 'Europe', p. 14.

20 'Unemployment Surges around the World, Threatening Stability', ibid.

21 For a remarkably dispassionate account of unemployed movements in the US by a participant, see Paul Mattick, *Arbeitslosigkeit und Arbeitslosenbewegung in den USA, 1929–1935* [1936] (Frankfurt, 1969), pp. 93ff. A particularly informative journalistic survey is Mauritz A. Hallgren, *Seeds of Revolt: A Study of American Life and the Temper of the American People During the Depression* (New York, 1933).

22 Mattick, *Arbeitslosigkeit*, p. 109.

23 Ibid., p. 114.

24 For a moving account, see 'Cacho', 'The Unemployed in the Popular Rising of December, 2001. Report from Greater Buenos Aires', in *International Journal of Political Economy*, XXXI/1 (2001), pp. 11–23. See also Aníbal Kohan, *¡A las calles! Una historia de los movimientos piqueteros y caceroleros de los '90 al 2002* (Buenos Aires, 2002) and 'Class Re-composition in Argentina', *Aufheben*, 11 (2003), pp. 1–23.

25 It was the practical Keynesian Hitler who first made May Day into an official holiday.

26 'The Seattle General Strike', in *Root and Branch: The Rise of the Workers' Movements*, ed. Root and Branch (New York, 1975), p. 209.

27 The classic theoretical reflection on this experience remains Anton Pannekoek, *Workers Councils* [1946] (Oakland, CA, 2003).

28 For a short look at the impact of the Great Recession on European agriculture, see Jean-Christophe Bureau, 'Agriculture européenne: les grands changements sont à venir', in CEPII, *L'économie mondiale 2010* (Paris, 2009), pp. 108–16.

29 German president Horst Köhler was forced to resign when he committed the unprofessional error of speaking the truth on a visit to German troops in Afghanistan: 'A country of our size, with its focus on exports and thus reliance on foreign trade, must be aware that military deployments are necessary in an emergency to protect our interests, for example, when it comes to trade routes, for example, when it comes to preventing regional

instabilities that could negatively influence our trade, jobs, and incomes': *International Herald Tribune* (1 June 2010), p. 3. On the other hand, Germany has also been forced to cut military spending in the effort to control its state deficit.

30 Tom Keefer, 'Fossil Fuels, Capitalism, and Class Struggle', *The Commoner*, 13 (2008–9), p. 15.

31 Ibid., pp. 19, 20.

32 Tom Keefer, 'Ownership, Depletion, and Control: National Oil Companies, Peak Oil, and the US Empire', unpublished manuscript. (2009), http://bildungsuerein.kpoe-steiermarkat/texts. phtml (last accessed 20 December 2010), p. 28, citing British Petroleum, BP *Statistical Review of World Energy* (June 2008).

33 José A. Tapia Granados, Edward L. Ionides and Oscar Carpintero, 'A Threatening Link Between World Economic Growth and Atmospheric CO_2 Concentrations', unpublished manuscript. (2009), http://sitemaker.umich.edu/tapia_granados/working_ papers_documentos_de_trabajos&config=ioUvVQoc8r2 DEUnkS988Ew (last accessed 20 December 2010), pp. 5–7.

34 Elizabeth Kolbert, *Field Notes from a Catastrophe: Man, Nature, and Climate Change* (New York, 2006).

35 For realistically grim speculations about the social and political consequences of climate change, see Gwynne Dyer, *Climate Wars: The Fight for Survival as the World Overheats* (Oxford, 2010)

36 Charles Fritz, 'Disasters and Mental Health: Therapeutic Principles Drawn from Disaster Studies', (Historical and Comparative Disaster Series 10) University of Delaware Disaster Research Center (1996), pp. 55, 57, 63.

37 Ibid., pp. 23–4.

38 Rebecca Solnit, *A Paradise Built in Hell*, cited in Rebecca Solnit, *A Paradise Built in Hell: The Extraordinary Communities that Arise in Disaster* (New York, 2009), pp. 107–9p. 162.

Acknowledgements

I have been discussing economic theory and the unfolding state of the economy with a number of friends for decades. In writing this book I received stimulation and information in particular from conversations with and editorial comments from John Clegg, Mary Lynn Cramer, Charles Reeve, Gary Roth, José A. Tapia Granados, Mariano Torras and Jeff Wilson. Katy Siegel first urged me to write the four articles for the *Brooklyn Rail* from which this book developed; without her encouragement I would probably never have done it. (Following the principle that no good deed can go unpunished, I asked her to give the manuscript for the present book a thorough reading; she made many improving suggestions.) Ted Hamm was a helpful editor at the *Rail*. The response to a French translation of the articles by Norbert Gobelin and Rémi Trom – *Le jour de l'addition: aux sources de la crise* (Paris: L'insomniaque, 2009) – helped convince me that a longer version of the argument would find readers, but it was the interest of Vivian Constantinopoulos at Reaktion that did the trick. Her editorial comments have also been invaluable. I thank her for waiting while a family emergency delayed production of the manuscript. Timing is necessarily difficult for a book focused as much as this one is on events whose details change from day to day, obscuring the more stable patterns analysis seeks to discern. As I assured her, however, the economic crisis will unfortunately last long enough to keep my theme of interest.

This book is for Jorge Valadas and, of course, for Katy, without whom nothing.